All Our Children

towards a NEW society

Published by Maurice Temple Smith
Ltd in association with New Society
Series Editor: Paul Barker

JACK TIZARD
PETER MOSS
JANE PERRY

All our children

Pre-school services in a changing society

TEMPLE SMITH/NEW SOCIETY

First published in Great Britain 1976
by Maurice Temple Smith Ltd
37 Great Russell Street, London WC1
© Jack Tizard, Peter Moss and Jane Perry
Typesetting by Red Lion Setters, London
Printed in Great Britain by
Billings Ltd, Guildford and London

ISBN   0 85117 0803 cased
        0 85117 0811 paperback

This series is published in association with
New Society; but the opinions expressed are the
responsibility of the authors and do not commit
the magazine as such in any way.

Contents

Editor's note

Anything written about children is also, by implication, about their parents. More precisely, it is about their mothers. (As this book points out right at the start, not enough thought has been given to the part that fathers play.) A study of pre-school care therefore faces a dilemma: whom are you most interested in helping — the mother, who has *her* needs, or the child, whose needs may not always be quite identical?

On the whole, the authors take the view that to help the mother *is* to help the child. But part of the strength of their text is that the data are there for those who might want to question this judgement.

Few subjects are guaranteed to generate more controversy than discussions of how good parents are at bringing up their own children. The idea of mothers going out to work while their children are young seems to make controversy fiercer. Once, working mothers were blamed for many of society's ills. Now the 'prison of the family' gets equally disproportionate blame.

We must never underestimate the skills of the 'amateur' — which etymologically means someone who loves what she or he is doing. The bonus that Benjamin Spock brought to parents was that, on the whole, they should rely on their own perceptions (not, say, those of Truby King) in bringing up their babies. The work of John and Elizabeth Newson in Nottingham has underlined how many ordinary parents always (for better or worse) continued to act as they saw fit, anyway.

But the authors are surely right to emphasise the diversity that should exist. And which has indeed existed in the past. I myself was brought up in a West Riding village where it was traditional for wives to have jobs. The workplace was not only a source of money, but also the nexus of all the local gossip. This is an area where motives are, very reasonably, mixed; and, provided there is no neglect, should be allowed for. *Paul Barker, New Society, 1976*

This is a book about the care and education of young children
in a changing society in which their needs, and the services
to provide for them, have recently become matters of great
political as well as psychological interest. It is also a book
about mothers. We should, but don't, say much about
fathers because it is mothers who bear the brunt of the
responsibility for child care, and because very little study
has been made of fathers' roles, either in the family or with
the children. This in itself is significant: sociologists and
psychologists have been much more interested in men as
workers than in men as husbands and fathers.

We have looked at early child care and education historically since only by doing so could we account for some of
the strange characteristics of our present day services, and
attempt to forecast future trends.

The care of children cannot be divorced from the needs
of families, from the demographic changes brought about by
family limitation and an increasing expectation of life, and
the rapid growth since the second world war of a consumer
society. These trends, and the rise in the standard of living
which has accompanied and in part caused them, have led
to changes in women's roles. Many more are working in paid
employment outside the home, and their role within the
home has changed. The nature of the family is changing too
and its functions are becoming more narrowly defined. We
ask ourselves, what is its future?

The changes that are occurring in Britain might seem to be
a passing phase specific to a single generation in a single
country, were it not that similar changes are occurring in all
industrial countries. They seem to be in response to needs
arising from economic and social developments. We raise the

question whether problems of providing nursery services can be settled except in the context of a more coherent social policy related to these more general social and economic changes.

At present services for young children are both inadequate and irrationally organised. What sort of serviees do we need — or want — and how can we best provide what we need or want? What is, and what should be, the role of professionals; how far should goals be set by them; how far by parents?

We argue that the aim of nursery services, indeed of all social and medical services, should be above all to improve the quality of life — and today the quality of life of many young mothers and young children is extremely poor. What can pre-school services do to improve it?

While we have been writing this book the economic situation has worsened and plans for the expansion of nursery services are already threatened. One of the few advantages of postponing an expansion of services is that it gives time to review development plans and ask ourselves whether what they promise is what we really want.

We have received much help in preparing this book from organisations and individuals. We should like to express our thanks in particular to the Department of Health and Social Security, the Department of Education and Science, and the Welsh Office for supplying us with unpublished information; to Westminster Social Services Department and Professor Neville Butler and A.F. Osborn of Bristol University, Department of Child Health, for letting us use unpublished data; to the embassies and other government departments of the European countries mentioned in the book, and Tom Schuller of the Centre for Educational Research and Innovation, OECD, for providing much material on foreign services; and to Dr Rick Heber of the University of Wisconsin for permission to quote extensively from recent publications of his. Among individuals, our thanks are due to Arthur and Margaret Wynn, and to Barbara Tizard, Gill Pinkerton, Martin Hughes and Olwen Davies of the Thomas Coram Research Unit.

1   Introduction

The last decade has seen an unprecedented growth of interest in young children, and in education and day-care services to meet their needs. In England the Plowden Committee (Central Advisory Council for Education, 1967) which considered *Children and Their Primary Schools* reported in some detail on the *educational* needs of 'pre-school' children and made recommendations as to how they should be met. A year later the Seebohm Committee (1968) devoted a substantial part of its *Report on Local Authority and Allied Personal Social Services* to consideration of *day care* services for young children, and the needs of their families.

Five years after the Plowden Report the government produced a White Paper, *Education: a Framework for Expansion*, in which it proposed a major expansion in nursery education. Educational provision for young children in Britain, was, it pointed out, very much less than that provided in many other industrial countries similar to our own. The White Paper noted that the 5 per cent of three year olds and 35 per cent of four year olds then receiving education in maintained schools were 'very low figures compared with the level of provision in some countries of the EEC' and backed this with examples from France (with nursery provision for 50 per cent of three year olds and 80 per cent of four year olds); Holland (over 80 per cent of four year olds); Belgium (80 per cent of three year olds, 90 per cent of four year olds) and Italy (50 per cent of three and four year olds).

The expansion in day care and education services for young children in some Western European countries is considered in Chapter 6. However, this expansion has not been confined to Western Europe as the following examples show:

Canada   Between 1956/6 and 1970/1, pre-school enrol-
ments rose by 54 per cent, attendance rates for three to five
year olds increasing from 17 per cent to 29 per cent;
expenditure in real terms was up by 110 per cent. Half the
present kindergarten places (for five year olds) were established in the 1960s and day-care places almost doubled
between 1967 and 1972 (OECD, 1973).

Czechoslovakia   Fifty-nine per cent of three to six year
olds attended kindergartens in 1972/3, the numbers having
doubled since 1945. In the 1960s, numbers at kindergartens
rose by a third, and day nursery places increased by 60 per
cent to provide for 12 per cent of the under three population
by 1972 (Brablcová et al, 1974).

Japan   The number of three to five year olds at private
and public kindergartens rose by 130 per cent between 1952
and 1962 and by a further 115 per cent in the next decade,
to 1.84 million. By 1972, 58 per cent of first year children in
elementary school had completed kindergarten (OECD, 1973).

New Zealand   Government policy has been directed to
expanding voluntary pre-school agencies, and the numbers of
children attending the two major ones — the Free Kindergarten
Union and the Play Centre Federation — increased sixfold
between 1945 and 1960, then more than doubled in the 1960s;
the number of centres provided by these agencies increased
from 370 to 1000 between 1960 and 1972. By 1972, over
53,000 children between the ages of 2½ and five (about one
third of the age group) were in play centres and kindergartens, mainly receiving part-time provision. A further 2,700
were in full-time day and factory nurseries, and though part-
time services will continue to expand with increased government aid, day nurseries now form the fastest growing sector
of provision (OECD, 1973).

Soviet Union   In 1960, the proportion of pre-school
children in creches and kindergartens was around 10 per cent.
Since then, construction of pre-school facilities has been
increasing at 'a furious rate', and by 1972 just over half of all
pre-school children were attending them (*Guardian* report,
16 October 1974).

The rapid, world-wide expansion of pre-school services is
an important and interesting phenomenon in its own right,

involving the extension of public services to a large group of highly dependent children. It raises issues of content, organisation and objectives, and problems concerned with relations with parents, with other services, and the community as a whole. But the significance of the expansion of pre-school provision goes beyond this. Advanced industrial societies are experiencing major demographic, economic, and social changes, many of which seem to be secular (that is, long-term) rather than cyclical or short-term. Associated with these changes are others connected with the aspirations, norms and beliefs of men and women in these societies. These latter changes, though less easy to quantify and define, are nevertheless very real and obvious. Changes in sexual *mores* associated with the growing acceptance and use of contraception and abortion; the development of the women's liberation movement; the concept of women's right to control their bodies and especially their reproductive functions, as a means to greater freedom and equality — these are just some of the developments associated with changing attitudes towards and among women and especially towards established concepts of female roles and life careers and the restrictions that these roles and careers impose.

The development of pre-school services, which we discuss in detail in later chapters, must be seen against the background of these demographic, economic, social and ideological changes, which both stimulate and are, in turn, facilitated by it. The exact relationships are sometimes not clear. However the rest of this chapter attempts to outline some of the more important of the underlying changes which are influencing not just the development of services but the whole pattern of family life and child-rearing, and in particular the role of women as wives, mothers and workers.

Marriage and the domestic career of the married woman
(Unless otherwise stated, the sources for the statistics given in the rest of this chapter are: 1971 Census Tables; Central Statistical Office (1975); Committee on One-Parent Families (1974); Office of Population Censuses and Surveys (1975 a and b). Information in this section of the chapter refers to England and Wales, but to Great Britain in the rest of the chapter.)

Since the 1930s, there has been a 'dramatic swing to higher probabilities of marriage and to consistently falling ages of marriage . . . the changes in marriage frequency and age since the 1930s [being] unequalled in any other period since the beginning of civil vital registration and probably in the past two or three centuries' (cited in Committee on One-Parent Families, 1974).

Between 1931 and 1974, the proportion of men (aged over fifteen) married at least once rose from 64 per cent to 75 per cent, while the increase for women was even more marked, from 65 per cent to 80 per cent. But the most marked change has been the fall in age of first marriages and the consequent increase in the proportions of younger age groups married, especially those under thirty; for instance the proportion of women aged twenty to twenty-four married at least once more than doubled from 1931 to 1971, from 26 per cent to 60 per cent. Overall, the average age of first marriage for bachelors dropped from 27.4 years in 1931-35 to 24.4 in 1970, rising slightly to 24.9 in 1974; for spinsters the change was from 25.5 years in 1931-35 to 22.4 in 1970 and 22.7 in 1974. The most marked increase has been in teenage marriages, with the proportion of first marriages under the age of twenty rising sixfold for bachelors between 1931-35 and 1974 and more than trebling for spinsters (to 10.5 per cent and 31.1 per cent respectively).

These developments have been accompanied by an increase in de jure marriage breakdown, expressed in more and younger divorces. The rate of decrees absolute granted per 1000 married population has risen from 2.1 in 1961 to 9.2 in 1974, an increase only partly explained by the new divorce legislation introduced in 1971. Moreover the proportion of marriages ending in divorce within their first ten years has risen from 3 per cent for those married in 1950/51 to 5.9 per cent for 1960/61 marriages, showing clearly the trend to more and earlier divorce; if the trend continues, the number of men who will marry more than once (due to widowhood or divorce) will rise from 12 per cent in 1976 to 20 per cent in 2001. Already, taking the widowed and divorced together, the proportion of all marriages involving one or both parties in remarriage rose from 16 per cent in 1964 to 29 per cent in 1974.

In addition to an increasing incidence of divorce all the evidence suggests that in recent years there has been a real rather than an illusory increase in all forms of marital disruption, that is de facto as well as de jure breakdown (Chester, 1972). Moreover the divorce rate (and probably the de facto breakdown of marriage also) in families with children has increased more rapidly than the rate of childless couples. In part because of this, the numbers of one-parent families with dependent children increased by 31 per cent between 1961 and 1971: during the same period the number of 'married couple' families with dependent children rose only 1 per cent. Another contributory factor in this increase in one-parent families has been a rising illegitimacy rate, illegitimate births being 5.1 per cent of all births in England and Wales in 1951 and 8.8 per cent of all births in 1974.

Overall, it has been estimated that in Britain there were 260,000 children under five in one-parent families in 1971 (rather over 5 per cent of the total under-five population), including 20,000 in motherless families.

Although, for the married woman, the chances of her marriage breaking down are increasing, the most significant and widespread changes in her domestic career are occurring in her experience of child-bearing. Married women have been having children younger and over a shorter period. Nearly two thirds of all legitimate births are now within five years of marriage while between 1951 and 1974 the proportion of legitimate live births accounted for by teenage mothers rose from 4.3 per cent to 10.7 per cent; in the same period, the proportion of births to women over thirty fell from 35.5 per cent to 19.8 per cent. Although a growing proportion of recent births have been illegitimate, the great majority are still within marriage even for teenagers. The proportion of teenage mothers who were married fell from 81 per cent in 1960 to 74 per cent in 1971, but the actual number of children born to them still rose substantially from 42,659 to 61,808.

Falling birth-rates, younger mothers and families spread over a shorter period are associated with changes in family size. Victorian families were typically large — but family size declined through the early decades of this century, reaching a low point in the 1930s. Although average family size increased again after the second world war, this was largely due to a decline in childlessness and a change from one to two and three-child families, rather than to an increase in the numbers of families with four or more children. Since the early 1960s, family size has again begun to drop, the average number of children after five years of marriage for women married in 1960-1964 and 1965-1969 being respectively 1.48 and 1.37.

The significance of this emergence of a stable pattern of low family size has been stressed by the Finer Committee:

> The achievement of the small, consciously planned family took place about the same time through the greater part of Western Europe and it must be reckoned a climacteric in social history. It is clear that neither variations in fecundity nor improvements in the manufacture and efficiency of contraceptives are causal explanations. The initiative and spread of family limitation appears to have been the response of married couples to social and economic changes, including the rising cost of preparing children to take their place in the adult world, which threatened an achieved standard of living.

The decline in family size has been closely related to the decline in overall birth-rates during the century. In 1974 the birth-rate in England and Wales was approximately 13 live births per 1000 population (below replacement level). This is only half the rate of the early 1900s and is considerably lower than the 18 per 1000 of the early 1960s, the most recent period of increasing birth-rates. Since 1964, there has been a strong downward trend, coupled with a sharp increase in the proportion of marriages remaining childless in their early years — 47 per cent of women married in 1970, aged twenty to twenty-four, were still childless after three years of marriage, compared to 34 per cent of those married in 1961.

The meaning and significance of this latest marked decline in birth-rate and increasing childlessness in early marriage is in dispute. The Office of Population Censuses and Surveys,

16

while recently lowering its future population projections, contends that basically people are postponing having children, and will eventually catch up, so that over their complete child-bearing cycle, they will have families very nearly as large as before the present decline. Its latest projection therefore allows for the present drastic fall in births to continue only until 1976 or 1977, when births will rise again partly due to increased fertility.

However, this reliance on interpreting recent birth-rates as mainly representing deferred births has been seriously challenged. Eric Thompson (1974) questioned the assumptions on which it is based, and has argued that the declining birthrate should be accepted as a new and significant trend in its own right which should be taken into account in preparing population projections. Whatever the pattern of fertility in the longer term, if net migration continues at its present rate, it seems likely that 1974 and 1975 will prove to have been years of no population growth: there may even have been a small drop in population.

One implication of all this is particularly relevant to married women. If fewer children are born and young adults continue to migrate, the labour force will be reduced. More children staying longer at school and more workers retiring earlier will have the same effect. As a consequence, increasing numbers of married women will probably continue to be needed in employment to make up for these losses.

The employment career of the married woman

In summing up the demographic and social changes outlined above, the Finer Committee concluded that 'longer life, a sex ratio near unity, more and younger marriages, with fertility compressed into a narrow band of years, has resulted in a revolutionary alteration in women's lives.'

As the Committee pointed out, one of the major consequences of this change has been its effect on the character of the female labour force. During and since the second world war there has been an unprecedented upward trend in the numbers of married women in paid employment, a trend in marked contrast to the declining contribution made by this group during the previous century. Between 1951 and

1971 the number of married women economically active rose by 118 per cent, to 5.8 million (42 per cent of all married women), and a further rise of 30 per cent has been estimated for the period up to 1986; the actual and estimated changes over the same two periods for 'other females' (unmarried women) are decreases of 21 per cent and 17 per cent, with increases in both cases of under 1 per cent for men. By 1971 married women already made up 23.1 per cent of the labour force, compared with 11.8 per cent in 1951, and the proportion is expected to continue growing.

This growth in married women's economic activity rates is due both to more married women having raised their families and returned to work at an earlier age, and to increasing numbers of mothers with dependent children going out to work. The situation of mothers with pre-school children is described in detail in Chapter 7. There it is shown that they have fully participated in this trend towards increasing employment, the numbers of such mothers in employment having risen by nearly a quarter of a million between 1961 and 1971: indeed during this decade the growth in the economic activity rate for married women with pre-school children was faster than for any other group of married women. This rapid growth rate has not been confined to Britain, but has occurred in most industrial countries.

In Britain, as in some other Western European countries, we thus face an unusually complex labour problem. The overall size of the potential labour force is likely to remain static, or decline as fewer children are born; younger adults are likely to continue to emigrate at current or higher rates: children are staying longer at school and in further education; and adults are retiring earlier. In this situation, with non-married women decreasing in numbers and virtually full employment among men, married women provide the only substantial reserve of labour.

Women's employment has benefited from changes in the structure of the economy and its labour force which have been occurring since the beginning of the century and especially since the second world war:

... between 1911 and 1966 the number of white-collar workers increased by 176 per cent ... [within which group] clerical occupations grew by 292 per cent ... while the number of manual workers increased by only 5 per cent, having actually decreased in total since 1931. The proportion of women among manual workers generally in 1966 was much the same as in 1911 ... the proportion of women has increased most dramatically in white-collar occupations, from 29.8 per cent in 1911 to 46.5 per cent in 1966 (Halsey, 1972a).

Women have been playing an increasingly important part in those commercial and service sections of the economy which have grown and will continue to grow in importance relative to the traditional and mainly heavy-industrial sectors where women have had little involvement, with a few exceptions such as textiles. Structural changes still going on in the nation's economy and employment needs are therefore contributing to the rising numbers of married women going out to work.

As well as trends in industry and the economy at large, the needs and attitudes of married women themselves are undergoing changes which encourage growing numbers to go to paid work. Opposition to the idea of working wives, especially among husbands, which became so influential in the Victorian era, has been breaking down — and today the phrase 'working mother' is slowly losing its pejorative overtone. Women are less willing to be confined solely to the care of house and children which, without the variation and break that employment provides, increasing numbers find stressful and lonely. In an age of increasing inflation and higher material expectations, wives going out to work provide one way of ensuring a continuing rise in family living standards or, at the least, their stability.

Education and employment
Today, as in the past, employed women continue to be concentrated in a limited range of occupations and industries.

In 1971 over two-thirds of women in employment were in the service industries and more than half in three particular groups — the distributive trades, professional and scientific services, and miscellaneous services such as catering and laundries. Similarly in manufacturing, women were mainly employed in four particular groups of industries — food, drink and tobacco, electrical engineering and clothing, footwear and textiles. There was no similar concentration among male employees (Central Statistical Office, 1974).

Women workers also in general hold positions involving less responsibility, skill and pay. The large numbers of women in the least skilled and responsible jobs, and indeed their increasing share of this part of the labour market, can be clearly seen by comparing the 1961 and 1971 figures for unskilled manual workers and junior non-manual workers. During that period, while the number of men in these two categories fell by 341,000, the number of women rose 728,000, this rate of increase being faster than the overall increase in female employment during the decade. As a consequence, women's share of these categories rose from 51 per cent to 58 per cent, while by comparison, women in 1971 provided only 37 per cent of the total labour force. Women's problem in breaking out of this position of inferiority is exacerbated by the growing number of women with dependent children entering the labour market, most of whom are forced into part-time employment, which is particularly liable to be of low skill and status.

However, women are making limited gains in higher status work and since 1961 the situation — at least in the higher professional and management occupations — shows a gradual change. Between 1961 and 1971, the number of women classed as employers, managers or professional workers rose from 359,000 to 487,000, this rate of increase being slightly faster than for all women in employment; there are still, however, over five times as many men in these higher occupational groupings.

This upward trend in women's employment reflects the increasing educational opportunities for girls. Thus in the United Kingdom, the number of full-time women undergraduates rose from 26,000 in 1961/2 to 65,000 in 1972/3, and in higher education as a whole, full-time and part-time women students grew by 69 per cent from 1965/6 to 1972/3, compared to 30 per cent for men. As mothers with higher education are more likely than other mothers to return to work when their children are still under five, this growth in women's higher education has considerable implications.

These should however not be overstressed, for women still experience substantial educational limitations and inequality, and much of their potential is still untapped.

Women undergo less education and training than men both during and after school. The educational trend generally has been a rising one and there has been a tendency for the gap between the sexes to narrow. . . . However in the 25-34 age group, who towards the end of the century will be assuming most of the most responsible positions in our society, only 2 per cent of women as against 7½ per cent of men have university degrees or equivalent qualifications . . . and the proportions (if other qualifications normally gained after 18) are also considered are 9.6 per cent and 12.9 per cent respectively. In 1971, three-quarters of all qualified women had their qualifications in education and health subjects, while qualified men had studied a much wider range of subjects (Central Statistical Office, 1974).

Mobility and the extended family

Other social changes, the effects of which are difficult to evaluate, arise from family mobility and the decline of the extended family. Increasing occupational change, slum clearances and rehousing cause families to move to new estates or new towns, or just to move to get more space or to live nearer the job. In consequence the household unit nowadays typically comprises two rather than three or four generations, and relatives are as likely to live many miles away as down the road or upstairs. Social contact, advice and support from relatives and friends are less easy to come by and social isolation and strain are more likely to occur.

It has also been argued that the social experience of the child is adversely affected by this change in the nature of his family:

> ... whatever the advantages offered by the smaller unit, it certainly affords fewer experiences in the process of socialisation, in terms of contact within the family with a variety of personalities and outlooks. Improvements in housing and the introduction of the mass media can further contribute to the isolation of the modern family from personal contact and have correspondingly accentuated the need for organised association, especially between children (Central Advisory Council for Education, 1967).

Writing nearly twenty years ago Willmott and Young (1957) gave a graphic picture of the way in which the class and family solidarity of an East London community was being destroyed by the rehousing of many of its younger adults in a newly built suburb. The description of the old working-class slum was perhaps nostalgic: too little may have been said of its negative features — the parochialism of a close, static community, the intergenerational conflicts and interference that close association must have brought in the post-war world, the lack of privacy as well as of physical amenities. Certainly many mobile families, especially perhaps middle-class ones with longer experience of this way of life and possibly more accumulated skill in making new contacts outside the family and immediate neighbourhood, seem not to suffer unduly, managing to maintain regular if less intensive contact with relatives distributed over a wide area. For all that, the account of the collapse of a community brought about by rehousing and dispersal rings true. It is difficult to draw up a balance-sheet of gains and losses: what is clear is that both occur, and that the changes which give rise to them are accelerating.

Ideological transition

The changing society in which pre-school services are also changing and developing is likewise characterised by changes in its ideologies. Traditional values, roles and principles are under increasing attack, and beliefs long regarded as

22

self-evident are held with less self-confidence. As has happened in other 'transitional' periods of history, new forms of social action, based on new concepts rather than traditional ones, are causing us to rethink the ideological premises we construct to explain and justify the social order.

In Eastern Europe, the decline in old values and roles has been a response to a consciously mounted, government supported attack, based on Marxist ideology:

A sustained and forceful effort [has] been made to bring women into business and social leadership . . . the family holds the key place in Marxist thinking as the basic cell of society . . . but it cannot perform its functions to best advantage so long as mothers are restricted to the role simply of housewife . . . . 'Mere' housewives are seen by Marxist thinkers as being subjected in capitalist society to double alienation. They are not independent, but in a sense the property of their husbands . . . and they are shut off from the main stream of work and social interchange, the means used by human beings to make themselves fully human (Fogarty, Rapoport and Rapoport, 1971).

In the West, similar attacks have been launched. The Women's Liberation Movement for example sees the prevailing industrial ideal·of division of labour and specialisation of functions as imprisoning wives and mothers in their homes and denying them individuality and equality. The necessity and value of the sharp differentiation of male and female roles in work, housekeeping, child-rearing and other aspects. of family life, and the inequitable and repressive situation of women which accompanies the present distribution of roles, have been thrown into question. Some dispute the value and desirability of the normative nuclear family, not just for women, but for all members including children — for according to this view the family is restrictive, repressive and anti-social.

These newly developing ideologies may be regarded in part as attempts to explain and validate widespread social developments whose impact can be seen most clearly perhaps in the United States. There, according to Bronfenbrenner

(1975), the progressive fragmentation and isolation of the family in its child-rearing role has been most rapid among younger families with younger children. The changes have increased with industrialisation, reaching their maximum among low-income families living in the central core of the largest cities. However, Bronfenbrenner adds, the general trend applies to all strata of society. Middle-class families in cities, suburbia and non-urban areas are changing in a similar way; and in terms of such characteristics as the proportion of working mothers, the (declining) number of adults in the home, single-parent families, or children born out of wedlock, the middle-class family of today 'increasingly resembles the low-income family of the early 1960s'.

It could be that the family as a social institution in the form in which we know it is changing to new and different forms of social bonding. If this were to happen it would indeed have profound consequences for child upbringing. However to consider these would take us into futurology — a field in which we have no competence. We therefore raise the issue here not to discuss it but to draw attention to the possible developments which, if they occur, will add new dimensions to the problems of child care.

The growing influence of professionals
The family has been under growing pressure from professional workers in health, education and welfare. The current development of pre-school services can be seen both as a consequence of and stimulus to control by professional and other interest groups. With this has come growing public deference to the influence and views of experts and a further shift in the balance of power between the family and professional workers in the sphere of child-rearing. In short, we are seeing, in the expansion of child-care services, an expression of the professional ideal which has stimulated and helped to organise social reform for over a hundred years. This professional ideal is the very antithesis of the universal, unlettered and haphazard nature of parenthood.

In view of the tension between professionalism and parenthood, it is not surprising that growing professional influence has led to increasing discussion and emphasis on the

24

lack of preparation for parenthood, the inadequacy of many parents to rear young children and their inability to meet all their needs and, at an extreme level, the gross physical and psychological harm done to children by some parents. Two aspects of this whole process are of particular interest. First, the explicit support for the institution of 'the family' combined with a widespread discussion of its present failing, leads to the advocacy of an emasculated form of the family rather than to a new social institution. And secondly, the process displays a confidence in the knowledge that professionals understand how children should be reared and that they are effective in their contribution to this rearing.

The strength of professional influence and interest in the care and upbringing of young children also reflects a growing belief in the unique importance of the early years to a child's future development and of the long-term damage that may arise from deprivation and other traumas in this period. Of particular influence has been current psychological theory which stresses (perhaps wrongly) that what happens to a child when he is young is likely to have long-term effects. This belief has greatly influenced American practice: both the early enthusiasm for the Head Start programme of services for three, four and five year olds, and the subsequent cry that Head Start had failed because IQs were not for the most part raised, were based on the beliefs about the over-riding importance of these early years for long-term goals.

The official view taken in Britain in setting the objectives for the expansion of nursery education is perhaps more modest, but is still concerned largely with ambitious, mainly longer-term goals. Nursery education may promote 'social development' and 'educational progress', including the use of language, thought and practical skills — 'progress of this kind gives a child a sound basis for his subsequent education' (Department of Education and Science, 1972).

Influenced by theories of the importance of early development, and hopes for its long-term effectiveness, the modern state is increasingly ready to accept that the progress of the pre-school child is too important to the future interests and needs of society to be left to parents. In the expansion of state-financed pre-school provision throughout industrial societies, we thus see the completion of the change, begun in the last century, which committed the state increasingly to take over or augment the role of educating and socialising children, as a means to increase efficiency and productivity, to strengthen the social order and meet the requirements of the labour market.

The case for nursery expansion

We would like to declare two prejudices that have influenced us in writing this book. The first concerns the goals of pre-school provision and the reasons for making such provision. It may be true, though as we point out in Chapter 10, the evidence is not as strong as many would have us believe, that early education and good child-care can produce long-term educational, social and other benefits for children and society. It is undoubtedly true that such outcomes are desirable and that efforts should be made to attain them. However the primary reason for providing good care for young children is, in our view, a short-term one. Good services increase the possibilities for happiness and well-being of young children and their families; and these immediate benefits are worthwhile and important. Given the amount of unhappiness and stress among young children and parents, at what should be a happy and enriching time of life, action to improve their lot is to be welcomed.

Secondly, in developing pre-school provision, we think that much more attention must be paid to changes occurring in society and to what people want. In other words the services should offer parents and children realistic alternatives from which to select those that best satisfy their changing needs and aspirations.

If offered a choice, it is clear that some mothers and fathers would wish to share child care, housework and employment, whilst others would wish to take it in turn over the years to accept the main responsibility for these various activities. In other families the mother would choose to retain the major responsibility for the children and home, though she might also wish to work away from home, at least part-time. In still other families traditional parent roles might be exchanged. Finally the mother — or for that matter the father — might remain at home full-time; or both parents might work full-time. Each of these ways of life offers its own rewards and exacts its own costs; and what will suit one family will not suit another. We wish to see parental choices made explicit and available.

Choices for parents imply choices for children — and our belief is that the choices for very young children are likely to be best made by their parents. Of course society can and should assist parents to make wise choices just as society can and should intervene when parents do harm to their children. But in general we see society's role as facilitative rather than restrictive; and we advocate an adequate provision of services because it is only in this way that we can offer real choices.

Many people who would agree in principle with this viewpoint oppose the expansion of out-of-the-home daytime services for young children because they believe that it is harmful for young children to spend all day, or even a few hours, in the care of adults who are not their primary parent figures. This view has for long been used as an argument against nursery expansion.

As we point out later, we think that the issues of maternal deprivation and maternal separation have become clouded by confusions between day care and residential care, and by unwarranted generalisations made on the basis of research carried out in institutions in which the quality of care is very poor. Our own view is that day care of good quality (and we can specify what we mean by that) is likely to benefit rather than harm young children.

We do not, at this point, wish to argue in more detail the issues of maternal deprivation. To prevent misunderstanding we do however wish to make explicit our view about the effects upon children attending a good day centre. To start with, there is, for example, widespread agreement that from the age of about three nearly all children enjoy and benefit from association with other young children; and there is abundant evidence that most cope happily with full-time nursery schooling even without their mothers. Where opinion differs is as to the effects of nursery attendance upon younger children, and as to the value of nursery care which lasts throughout a full working day.

We believe that many younger children would benefit from attendance at a well-run nursery centre for part or even most of the day; and we think very few indeed would be harmed by it (they could be kept home if they weren't happy). This does not mean that we think all young children *ought* to attend a nursery centre, any more than we think all mothers ought to go out to work. Probably many more mothers *would* go out to work if they knew their children were being properly cared for in their absence. Probably, too, many more children would spend longer periods in day care if day care services were available. But many mothers would prefer, as the playgroup movement has shown, to share their delight in bringing up young children with other mothers and other children. And many others would keep their children at home. What we are saying is that good services make it possible for parents to make such choices; in doing so they promote wellbeing in a way that cannot be attained by other means.

Social conditions, patterns of employment and housing, family structure and roles are changing, and if we retain an out of date pattern of services, we are forcing many families to make arrangements that are inadequate and unsatisfactory both for children and parents. To secure the optimal conditions for the care and upbringing of young children, government itself must act.

2 The nineteenth century: early childhood in an era of growth

The roots of change in attitudes to young children and mothers, and in services for them, lie in the industrialisation of Britain. In this chapter and the next, we therefore begin by describing social conditions and customs in the nineteenth century, especially as they affected women and children, and the ideas about childhood and education that were emerging.

In fact we know little about how young children lived and were raised in the nineteenth century, or about the lives of their parents, especially their mothers. But from official statistics (for example the Census, the Reports of the Registrar-General), from the evidence given to Royal Commissions and official Committees, and towards the end of the century from the new wave of social and statistical studies which marked the Victorian's desire to understand his world more clearly, we learn much about the harshness and cruelty to which numberless children were subjected.

In other respects our knowledge of how young children lived in the nineteenth century is almost as sketchy as our knowledge of life in Stuart times:

In the pre-industrial world there were children everywhere;
... [yet] these crowds and crowds of little children are
strangely absent from the written record ... there is
something mysterious about the silence of all these
multitudes of babes in arms, toddlers and adolescents in
the statements men made at the time about their own
experience. Children appear of course but so seldom and
in such an indefinite way that we know very little about
child nurture. (Laslett, 1965).

Our ignorance of the past would be more surprising if the

manner in which young children and their parents live today were better documented — but there are remarkably few detailed accounts, such as that by John and Elizabeth Newson of child-rearing in Nottingham, to give future generations a concrete idea of what it was like to be a child, and of how parents behaved to children, in the middle of the twentieth century.

Death and disease in nineteenth-century England

Perhaps the most stark aspect of nineteenth-century life was the appalling death-rate for children under five, and especially under one. This remained high throughout the whole of the century, even showing a tendency to rise after 1850. In contrast, the health of the rest of the population improved, and the death rate fell throughout most of the century: it was, indeed, this fall in the death rate which was largely responsible for the phenomenal growth in population.

As late as 1904 the Interdepartmental Committee on Physical Deterioration expressed their concern that, though general death-rates had fallen considerably in the previous 25 years, infant mortality had not. On the contrary, deaths during the first year of life had risen from 148 per 1000 in 1841-5 to 156 per 1000 in 1851-5 and they still averaged 153 per 1000 between 1891 and 1900; only in the present century did the rate drop, reaching 105 in 1910 and maintaining a steady decline to present-day figures of under 17. (Rosen, 1968; Halsey, 1972a). And the annual death-rate of children aged one to four stayed at between 60 and 70 per 1000 until the 1880s, when it too began to fall steadily if not dramatically.

Average figures for deaths hide large variations. Mortality rates were highest of all in towns, especially large ones (Preston, Burnley and Blackburn, for instance, had infant mortality rates of over 200 between 1890 and 1900) and lowest in rural areas; and though infant deaths occurred in all social classes, the greatest number occurred among children of manual workers and the poor.

Accompanying and partly responsible for this terrible toll were high levels of ill health, especially from infectious diseases, some of which were particularly virulent in the

30

middle of the century. Severe and frequent epidemics of scarlet fever between 1840 and 1880 made it a leading cause of death among the infectious diseases of childhood; two-thirds of its victims were children under five, an average of 7 per 1000 dying annually of the fever from 1859 to 1885. A serious epidemic of diphtheria occurred in the 1840s, and another in the 1890s, and this too was primarily a scourge of childhood.

Urbanisation and population growth

High morbidity and mortality rates were particularly associated with urban life; and the nineteenth century saw an unparalleled growth in urbanisation. By 1851 'for the first time in modern history, a body politic had got into a mainly urban condition' (Best, 1971). Within a rapidly growing population — which rose from 8.9 million in 1801 to 36 million in 1911 — an ever-growing proportion squeezed into towns. These simply did not cope with the increasing demands for the services and organizations that this growth required if living conditions and health were not to suffer.

Within a hundred years, the situation at the start of the century, when only a fifth of the population were true town dwellers, had been totally reversed. Examples show the pressure faced by urban areas. During the first fifty years of the century, Manchester increased from 85,000 to 400,000; Leeds from 53,000 to 172,000; Bradford from 13,000 to 104,000; Sheffield quadrupled in size; and Birmingham trebled. Although the rate of growth slowed in the second half of the century, the urban population increased by over 20 per cent every decade from 1851 to 1881, by which time over a third of the population lived in 20 urban areas of 100,000 or more people. Infant mortality, a sensitive indicator of community health, showed the influence of poor environmental conditions such as bad housing and especially over-crowding, inadequate sanitation, poor food and polluted water; its dismal history in this period indicates clearly the extent of the failure to cope with urban growth.

Poverty and the family

Poor living conditions went hand in hand with widespread

Figure 1: Growth of Population of England & Wales

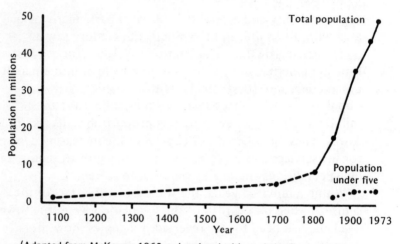

(Adapted from McKeown 1965 and updated with statistics from censuses and Registrar General's returns.) See Table 1.

and endemic poverty and a growing inequality of income within and between classes. The extent of absolute poverty which emerged from the pioneer social surveys at the end of the century, shocked even the researchers. Both Booth (in London from the 1880s) and Rowntree in York in the 1890s estimated that 3 in 10 of the population were in poverty; and an estimate for 1867 implies a figure of 35 per cent for the country as a whole (Perkin, 1969). In human terms, these figures meant that nearly every unskilled and agricultural worker and his family lived on the fringe of subsistence, while in the recurrent periods of trade depression, with widespread wage cuts, short-time work and unemployment, many more workers, including some of the more skilled, were dragged down to this level.

Particularly vulnerable were families with small children. Rowntree identified this phase in the worker's life (with lowered family earnings and increased costs) as one of the worst troughs in the cycle of poverty he described. The vulnerability of young families is shown in a study of three towns — Oldham, Northampton and South Shields — where in 1849 (a relatively prosperous year)

> the incomes of an outright majority of working families were already too low for them to buy all the food they needed, or would have been if they had had to support just one extra adult member. Moreover these figures refer only to primary poverty. The larger reality of additional poverty caused by illegitimacy, unemployment and debt were very much worse . . . In all three towns, poverty was a regular feature of the life of almost all working families at certain stages in their development, especially in old age or before young children could start to earn (Foster, 1974).

The only solutions for families faced by such privation were to starve slowly, to send mothers and children to work, or to share housing with relatives or others. Sharing meant gross overcrowding and encouraged disease, but as the three-town survey showed, this was forced on 40 per cent of Northampton labourer families, 50 per cent of Oldham families and 72 per cent of South Shields families — and these must have been typical findings.

Squalid though life was in town, it was worse in the country, and throughout the century vast numbers of people left the rural areas simply to find work in towns and cities. True, the rural environment might have been healthier in some respects — infant mortality was somewhat lower — but otherwise the lot of the agricultural labourer and his family, especially in the South, was atrocious for most of the century. Earnings were amongst the lowest in the country, far below what was offered in the new factories; housing was often appalling (with rural authorities particularly reluctant to use their housing powers); and unemployment, especially during the first half of the century and outside harvest time, was rife. Rural childhood might include some compensations, notably more pleasant surroundings, but it was still hard and far from child-centred, even in the 1880s:

> Around the hamlet cottages played many little children too young to go to school. Every morning they were bundled into a piece of old shawl, a slice of bread was thrust into their hands and they were told to 'go play' while their mothers got on with the housework. In winter, their little limbs purple-mottled with cold, they would stamp around playing horses or engines . . . they were like little foals turned out to grass and received about as much attention. They might, and often did, have running noses and chilblains on hands, feet and ear-tips, but they were hardly ever ill enough to stay indoors. 'Makes 'em hardy' their mothers said and hardy they became (Thompson, 1945).

At the other end of the social scale, comfortable housing, expensive education, proper day-care, a too-rich diet, numerous servants and a more than adequate income were available for the increasingly affluent families of the upper and middle classes (the 'top' 10 per cent of families shared about two fifths of national income in 1803 and over half by 1867). And though life for their young children, as we shall see, could still be very harsh, the British nanny being capable of great rigidity and even cruelty, this hardship was at least self-inflicted — by parents if not by their children.

Some better-paid workers, especially the relatively prosperous 'labour aristocracy' or skilled artisans, were also able to obtain, through higher income, some of the basic requirements of a healthy childhood. But the market economy, as a means to meet basic needs, was irrelevant to the great mass of working people, whose position in the first two-thirds of the century probably deteriorated in relation to other classes.

There were few attempts to combat the social ills suffered by most of the population. 'What was needed was an adequate family income; a higher standard of living including proper housing; a better diet including pure milk; knowledge of child care; and facilities to aid working mothers. None of these was present in the Victorian city as far as the workers and the poor were concerned' (Rosen, 1973). There were some attempts to help, but they were invariably impermanent, or too limited, or too late, or misconceived and badly done. Attempts at family income maintenance, geared to family size, were tried by some Poor Law Authorities in the early part of the century, especially in the South, but were hardly generous and were promoted as an alternative to higher wages. Some local authority interest in housing began towards the end of the century, but the results in terms of new public housing were very limited; too often housing reform was equated purely with demolition and not with rebuilding.

Improved nutrition, in the limited form of school meals provided from the 1860s by voluntary enterprise, was inefficiently organised, leaving most children and areas uncovered. And even after local authorities were given power in 1906 to provide meals, a mere 360,000 school children out of over 6 million were fed when the service reached its highest peak before the first world war. Apart from this, and some voluntarily organised milk depots, there were no public attempts to improve the quantity and quality of diet, despite an awareness of declining breast-feeding and the inadequacy of alternative milk or other diets.

School Health Services started in a small way at the end of the century (Bradford providing the first school medical inspection in 1891, and the first school medical clinic); but only 43 out of 322 education authorities had begun medical inspections by 1907 when legislation made this a local authority duty (Gilbert, 1966). There were of course medical services, both fee-paying and free, but no proper community and infant health service existed. Hence parents commonly turned to self-medication or sought the advice of druggists or quacks. In consequence, 'vast quantities of patent medicine are sold for every conceivable condition . . . one of the most injurious of these being a drink prepared with opiates, Godfrey's Cordial' (Engels, 1968 edition). This and other substances were frequently resorted to by parents and by child-minders to keep infants quiet, and one mid-century estimate in Preston put the number of families using the Cordial as 1,600, each family going through half-an-ounce a week (Rosen, 1973). No adequate study of the effects of dosing small children with such unsuitable drugs was made, but they were known to be pernicious.

Work and the idea of childhood

The prevailing attitudes and behaviour towards children seem to us today insensitive and callous. This was partly because of the normality of sudden and frequent childhood illness and death which

> for the whole of human history up to the turn of the present century has made simple physical survival the dominant issue in child upbringing. With death and the subsequent danger of damnation ever present, moral (together with physical) growth was the main preoccupation of many parents in respect to their children (Newson, 1974).

Parallel with this insecurity of childhood went the idea

> that childhood was not a separate state, but a period of defective adulthood, out of which children had to be trained as fast as possible . . . children were [seen as] little adults, but little adults with evil faults which had to be eradicated as soon as possible . . . [This idea] persisted strongly into Victorian and Edwardian times (Gathorne-Hardy, 1972).

The idea of childhood, as we think of it today, with its separation from the demands and experience of adult life, did develop during the century, but slowly. And the widespread involvement of children in the world of employment, which continued well into the second half of the nineteenth century, shows the importance of the other, less differentiated view of children and their place in society. Thus, for much of the century, the children of agricultural workers still worked in much the same way as their counterparts had done three hundred years before, 'from dawn to dusk in winter, from eight till six in the spring; and in harvest time often from five in the morning until nine at night' (Pinchbeck and Hewitt, 1973). Children of workers in small-scale domestic or cottage industry fared as badly or worse. From the time they could walk they too began to work, fetching and carrying.

The living and working conditions of children in the factories and mines were even more harsh and cruel. As Thompson (1963) puts it, nearly all the vices known to the eighteenth century were perpetrated in the early decades of the nineteenth but in an intensified form. The reports of the Children's Employment Commissions of 1842 showed that the Poor Law Guardians were still getting rid of pauper boys of six, seven and eight by 'apprenticing' them to colliers. They were

> wholly in the power of the butties and received not a penny of pay . . . and the mixture of terror and fatalism of the children comes through in the laconic reports. An eight year old girl employed for thirteen hours a 'day' to open and close traps: 'I have to trap without a light, and I'm scared . . . Sometimes I sing when I've light, but not in the dark. I dare not sing then.'

As for the factory system, it inherited the worst features of the domestic system in a context which had none of the domestic compensations: 'it systematized child labour, pauper and free, and exploited it with persistent brutality.' It was only during the second half of the nineteenth century, not the first, that the exploitation of child labour began to be effectively checked.

37

The lives of working-class mothers

'The typical working-class mother of the 1890s, married in her teens or early twenties and experiencing ten pregnancies, spent about fifteen years in a state of pregnancy and in nursing a child for the first year of its life. She was tied, for this period of time, to the wheel of child bearing' (Titmuss, 1958). Given this burden, and the continuous struggle to make ends meet, most mothers could hardly have had any time to devote to child-oriented activities, even had their importance been generally recognised. Child care was bound to be limited mainly to physical care, not just because of the stress on physical survival, but because this was all there was time for; and family and children's lives were organised to this end. Thus Flora Thompson's rural children were turned out 'like foals' each day to let their mothers do the housework, and the only child in the family to receive much parental attention was the current baby, who was in turn relegated to the care of older sibs when the next baby came along. The tragedy of the situation for the nineteenth-century mother was that by the time she had finished with child care, she could expect to live only a further twelve years, probably in increasingly bad health.

Working mothers

One of the larger gaps in the nineteenth-century official statistics — indeed in all official statistics up to 1961 — is the failure to provide information on working mothers; in fact not until 1911 does the Census even make a distinction in its occupational tables between unmarried, married, and widowed women. The first official figures on married women working come from the 1851 Census, where the proportion of married women (including widows) in employment in Great Britain is given as 24 per cent — a figure not passed again until the 1950s. Before that date we are reduced to guessing trends. On this weak basis, it seems probable that the numbers of employed married women rose — absolutely if not necessarily relatively — in the first half of the century; textile factories and domestic industries connected with factory production increasingly used female labour, and in agricultural areas more women were forced to work when the 1834 Poor Law

Amendment Act removed the subsidies paid to married men to keep their families.

When the employment rate began to fall again is impossible to answer, but over the sixty years following 1851 the trend overall was downwards, so that by 1911 only between 13 and 14 per cent of married and widowed women (in England and Wales) were employed. The proportion stayed at about this level until the rapid increase after 1945. The reasons for this decline in married women working can again only be guessed, but major factors must have been increasing male earnings and a growing distaste for wives working — 'to have a wife who did not work outside the home became as important and assumed as symbolic a character for the self-respecting industrial worker as for the middle-class husband' (Klein, 1965). Changing industrial conditions also played their part, the early nineteenth-century period of rapid growth in the cotton industry — in which women took a major role — being superseded by rapid growth in engineering, steel, mining and transport, where women never gained a foothold; and in agriculture, higher wages and more mechanisation contributed to a decline in female labour.

However, the position of married women's employment was not uniform. The 1901 and 1911 censuses showed employment rates to be twice as high in urban as rural areas, and within urban areas, low rates were found in mining, engineering and seaport towns. Rates were particularly high in textile areas (Burnley, Blackburn, Macclesfield, Darwen and Preston, for instance, all had over 30 per cent of married and widowed women in employment); pottery towns (Burslem 22 per cent, Longton 31 per cent); and in a few other towns with traditional female-employing industries (for example, Luton with 40 per cent). The main industries in which married women worked, accounting for well over half of those aged 20 to 34, were textiles, dressmaking, laundering, and shopkeeping and dealing.

These regional variations emphasise that, as is the case today, it is difficult to generalise about women and particularly married women's employment. Married women in the Lancashire cotton industry for instance were the best paid female workers in the country, and in work such as weaving they enjoyed virtual parity of pay with men. They worked in factories, belonged to strong trade unions and, barring general depressions, enjoyed steady employment. By contrast, in London, because of the relatively high earnings of skilled and semi-skilled men, wives normally did not work. Women in general only worked from necessity, wives of men in the many seasonal and casual trades being forced to work fairly constantly. With a large labour glut, wage rates were very low, employment irregular, trade unions virtually unknown; and the bulk of the work done by married women was home work.

Some of the fullest information about women in employment, and especially mothers, is furnished in the Report of the Interdepartmental Committee on Physical Deterioration (1904) which includes a memorandum on the employment of mothers in factories and workshops prepared by the Principal Lady Inspector of Factories. The reasons for working given by mothers of young children were reported to include fear of loss of future factory work, and preference for factory over domestic work; but the main causes were the death, unemployment or low wages of the husband. The lack of regular employment for men is also given as a major reason for the higher employment rates in Dundee, the Potteries and Preston, though the Inspector reporting on the Potteries notes that 'it is impossible not to be impressed by the universal preference amongst women for factory over domestic life and how depressed and out of health they become if obliged to remain at home.'

Despite the decline in married women in employment, and despite the fact that the number of employed mothers could never have been more than a minority of all mothers, the working mother was a cause of much concern and criticism throughout the century. Over and above the general distaste for women working, much of the criticism and concern focused on the effects of mothers working on their children, especially their infants. Engels (1968 edition) raged against the consequences of employment of women in factories which

breaks up the family, for when the wife spends twelve or thirteen hours every day in the mill, and the husband works the same length of time there or elsewhere, what becomes of the children . . . the general mortality among young children must be increased and is placed beyond doubt by notorious facts.

The 1851 Census report echoes this concern:

the duties of a wife, mother and a mistress of a family can only be efficiently performed by unremitting attention; accordingly it is feared that in districts where women are much employed from home, the children and parents perish in great numbers.

The 1904 Interdepartmental Committee on Physical Deterioration in its turn 'had no doubt that employment of mothers in factories is attended by evil consequences to themselves and their children and would gladly see it diminished'.

Given the general conditons of Victorian towns and the total inadequacy of satisfactory day-care provision for young children of working mothers, it is not surprising that these children (and especially the very young ones who were the main subjects of official concern) suffered unduly, at least as measured by infant mortality rates, for 'whether the mothers of young children worked in the mills of Lancashire, the Staffordshire Potteries or in the fields of Lincolnshire, the infant mortality rate was markedly higher in their families than in those of mothers who did not work' (Perkin, 1969). As if to prove the point, during the Lancashire cotton famine of 1861-4, when many textile workers were unemployed, infant mortality rates declined in the area. But in 1911 the infant mortality rates for the children of cotton workers still remained comparatively high — and Lancashire still had an almost total lack of services for employed mothers with young children.

Return to work after child-birth

A major danger to the health of mother and baby was caused by mothers returning to work too soon after the birth. Engels found that 'women often return to the mill three or four days after the confinement, leaving the baby of course;

in the dinner hour they must hurry home to feed the child and eat something and what sort of suckling that can be is evident ... the use of narcotics to keep the child quiet is fostered by this infamous system.' As late as 1891 it was necessary to bring in legislation which ruled that factory managements were not knowingly to employ a women within four weeks of birth, but in many cases this was not observed.

The main problem was the lack of adequate day-care facilities, which left mothers with a number of unsatisfactory options to choose from. Alternatives in Manchester of the 1840s were 'either to lock [the children] up or give them out to be taken care of' (Engels, 1968 edition). The situation was not greatly altered, especially for children under three, by the 1900s when the working mother often still had only two courses open to her — 'leave her children unattended ... or send them to be taken care of by a neighbour or professional "minder" ' (Board of Education, 1908). The Board of Education Consultative Committee on School Attendance for the under fives painted a black picture of child minding:

> ... for a neighbour's care, there is at best much to be said. The 'professional' minder is nearly always unsatisfactory. The Committee are informed that it is common practice in some districts for ignorant women to earn a living by minding neighbours' children. The minder takes an average of 8d a day. There is no inspection or control ... [they are] often dirty and unsatisfactory, often conducted by women of the grossest ignorance. It is common practice for children to be drugged.

Especially in the earlier part of the nineteenth century, the minder merges into the institution of the dame school, where as many small children as possible were crowded into a tenement or cellar 'usually unhealthy, dirty and Ill-ventilated; if the woman in charge had any formal education herself she might try to give some instruction in alphabet and reading during part of the long day' (Whitbread, 1972). During the second half of the century the growth of proper schools, and the increasing numbers of children under five attending them, provided an increasing alternative to the dame school or other minders — though not really for children under three.

However the picture was not entirely black and contemporary prejudices against working mothers may have blinded critics to the contributions made by other, better child-care arrangements. In Preston in 1851, for instance, 23 per cent of married mothers with children were employed, 52 per cent of them working in factories (a reminder that quite a number of mothers were still employed in their own homes). Nearly half of these 'factory' households included unemployed grandparents, other relatives or lodgers, who could have been available to care for the children (Anderson, 1971). The same author also notes that many other children would have been with relatives or friends living nearby, and concludes that if half the infant children of factory-employed mothers were cared for in their own homes and half of the remainder were with nearby relatives and friends, then less than 2 per cent of all infants in this industrialised district would have been left with paid minders.

Unfortunately for the minority of infants and older children who were not cared for by relatives or friends, there was no adequate institutional day-care alternative. Throughout the whole of the century child care had to be privately arranged and organised by parents, since very little was provided from any public or voluntary source. Thus the *first* day nursery in Britain was opened in St Marylebone, London, only in 1850, and admission was only to be secured on recommendation of a minister of religion or other respectable person. As the fees were high, the experiment was not a great success, and the few other similar nurseries established elsewhere in the country met with similar results.

More promising were two free kindergartens opened in Manchester in 1871 and 1872, followed by four in London; by 1906 there were thirty. These day nurseries provided adequate physical care, but could hardly make much impact on the need. The same can be said of the most notable event of the whole of the period — the opening in 1911 by Rachel and Margaret McMillan of their day nursery school in Deptford. This provided in a remarkable way for the physical, educational and social needs of children from the age of two to eight or nine. But despite Margaret McMillan's hopes that after the first world war her day nursery school would provide a model for a universal pattern of services for young children, this did not happen. For working mothers in general there was no such enlightened approach to the care of their children.

3 The rise and fall of early education

Reforms and new ideas

Compared with the phenomenal rate of demographic, economic and social change in the century preceding the first world war, the development of social and welfare services was timid and unremarkable. 'The nineteenth century,' says Bertrand Russell, (1934)

> was brought to its disastrous end by a conflict between industrial techniques and political theory. Machine production, railways, telegraphs and advances in the art of war, all promoted organisation, and increased the power of those who held economic and political command . . . But effective political thought had not kept pace with the increasing concentration of authority: theory, insofar as it had succeeded in moulding institutions, was still divided between monarchy and competitive democracy, the first essentially pre-industrial, and the second appropriate only to the earliest stages of industrialism. Plutocracy, the actual form of government in Western countries, was unacknowledged and as far as possible concealed from the public eye.

The greatest single advance in social legislation affecting children was the introduction of compulsory education in the 1870s. Other reforms came in piecemeal fashion and very slowly. Thus the first Factory Act to prevent nightwork and to limit to twelve the number of hours worked by 'pauper apprentices' (that is, pauper children 'apprenticed' to local factory owners whose virtual property they became until they were twenty-one) was passed as early as 1802. But it applied only to paupers and only to cotton — and it was completely ineffective. A second Act, passed in 1819 and also applying only to cotton, put the minimum age for employment in the mills at nine years, and limited hours to twelve a day for children under sixteen years of age. This too was completely ineffective, in that inspection was left to clergymen and magistrates who had no interest in the working conditions of children. Not until 1833 was the first effective Factory Act passed — and even that, as Cole and Postgate (1948) put it, was 'not very generous'. The Act dealt only with textiles, specifically excepting silk; it limited the hours of children under thirteen to eight, and under eighteen to twelve. But since only four inspectors were appointed to see that it was carried out, its effectiveness must also have been limited.

Amending legislation was passed in 1842 and 1844, but during the next twenty years the demands of the labour market for increased numbers of children, the administrative problems of the next stage of 'state interference' and all the moral and economic interests upholding the doctrine of 'the freedom of the subject' obstructed further progress until the late sixties, when there was a new spate of child protection legislation. So it was not until 1867 that it was made illegal for children under eight to work in gangs in the fields from dawn to dusk, often under the supervision of brutal overseers; and not until 1875 that the use of boys for sweeping chimneys was effectively prohibited. And only in the last quarter of the century, largely as a result of the efforts of voluntary societies, were the first steps taken to do something about the prevention of cruelty to children by their parents and in their own homes.

These and other laws to protect children against the abuses of employment, baby farming and parental cruelty, and also to encourage and finally demand education for them, began the system of legal safeguards protecting the rights of children. But a comprehensive system of child care and protective legislation and administration did not come into being until well into the present century.

Accompanying, and in part responsible for, the development of protective legislation during the latter years of the nineteenth century went the establishing of voluntary organisations to care for and to protect the destitute and neglected child — Dr Barnardo's; children's societies associated with various denominational groups; the Charity Organisation Society; the National Society for the Prevention of Cruelty to Children (not founded, incidentally, until sixty years after the Royal Society for the Prevention of Cruelty to Animals).

But when the question of legal reform and statutory powers became a live issue, nineteenth-century attitudes towards child protection often seem curiously ambivalent to our eyes today: they reflect the conflicts faced by the beneficiaries of laissez-faire when attempting to remedy its defects. Thus Shaftesbury, for all his concern with chimney sweeps and factory children, opposed proposals for compulsory education on the grounds that they were a distinct infringement of the rights of the parents to bring up a child as they thought fit, and as such could only encourage dependence on the State at the expense of personal initiative and responsibility. For the same reason he opposed, in 1871, legislation designed to offer a modicum of protection against parental cruelty. Likewise the Charity Organisation Society, though greatly concerned with the wellbeing of the poor, opposed proposals made at the end of the century for the introduction of school meals for grossly malnourished children. The Society held that 'it is better in the interests of the community to allow the sins of the parents to be visited on the children, than to impair the principle of the solidarity of the family and run the risk of permanently demoralising large numbers of the population by offering free meals to their children' (Pinchbeck and Hewitt, 1973).

This obsessive fear of demoralising the poor through indiscriminate charity or services, epitomised by the Charity Organisation Society's policies, acted as a powerful brake against any large-scale public initiative in the crucial areas where such initiative was needed. And in the absence of more basic and comprehensive measures, such benevolent developments as occurred in the nineteenth century made only a marginal effect on the lives (and deaths) of most small children.

There were however other forces for change more powerful

than the ideas of reformers and educationalists. A growing concern for the plight of the poor, by social researchers in the 1880s and the general public, was leading to a call for reform. So too was the fear of violence and revolution and of a working class that became increasingly alienated from the middle and upper classes throughout the century. For 1886 and 1887 were years of general depression and high levels of unemployment, which gave rise to violent riots in London. Middle-class fear of the casual poor, the despised 'residuum', gained new credibility, and the experience of rioting mobs, smashing property in the heart of the metropolis, bred very real expectations of actual insurrection. Then in 1889, a second wave of trade union organisation among unskilled and semi-skilled workers swept the country (there had been an earlier wave in the early 1870s); a series of strikes culminated in a successful dock strike that completely shut the Port of London. A small but increasing number of socialists played an active part in much of this unrest, which was followed in the 1890s by further industrial trouble, this time with established trade unions, and there were major strikes in the cotton, mining and engineering industries. The formation of the Independent Labour Party, pledged to socialism, was followed by the establishment of the Labour Representation Committee in 1900 to increase the number of Labour MPs, and finally in 1906, when 29 members of the LRC were elected to Parliament, the Committee was renamed as the Labour Party, with its MPs constituted as a proper parliamentary party.

Industrialism had eventually led to an organised labour movement which forced the two major parties to give higher priority to social reform, both to preserve their working-class vote and to win support from labour organisations. In this they were partially successful. Even so:

the period from 1900 to 1914 is like the first two acts of a play whose third act was never written. The historian can trace the breaking up of the Victorian Age, its castes, taboos, commercial methods and social habits, and the development, isolated or allied, of various movements of revolt. But when the struggle develops and it seems that some sort of denouement must come, the action is violently and suddenly stopped. Within a day almost — a week at the longest — in August 1914, the whole of men's preoccupations and thoughts was wiped out (Cole and Postgate, 1948).

Doubts about Britain's ability to maintain her industrial and imperial pre-eminence, and a growing awareness of the developing power of other countries, had been increasing through the second half of the nineteenth century. An educated population became a national necessity if foreign competition was to be held off. Hence educational reports towards the end of the century are full of comparative figures and descriptions of foreign educational practice. And though the disclosures of poverty by Booth and Rowntree had had little direct effect in government circles, the crucial importance of a fit and healthy people, and how far the country was from such a goal, was brought home by the Boer War. The Director-General of the Army Medical Service during the Boer War reported that the Inspector of Recruiting was having great difficulty in obtaining sufficient men of satisfactory physique for service in the Forces: 40 per cent of volunteers were rejected for heart afflictions, poor sight and hearing, and bad teeth, and this despite a reduction in the minimum height for recruits to five feet (Burnett, 1968). The resultant alarm led to the establishing of an Inter-Departmental Committee on Physical Deterioration and the conversion of a rather casual public interest in the health of school children into sudden, widespread fear of physical degeneration among the British working class. 'A healthy working class child was priceless in a way he had not been before . . . one result was a proliferation of infant welfare centres and milk depots in the poor areas of London' (Gilbert, 1966). Not only did all this reinforce the position of the reformers already in the field, but fear of physical deterioration of the national stock and the slogan of 'national efficiency' enabled Conservative imperialists to fall in behind the call for social reform.

A mixture of fear and disquiet on the part of the upper classes, and a growing working-class organisation and strength, aided by the efforts of a committed band of civil servants and social reformers, prepared the way for the burst of reforms of the 1900s which laid the foundations of the modern Welfare State.

In conjunction with growing anxiety about the decline of Britain's industrial supremacy, apprehensions about the depopulation of the countryside and uncertainty about the future political role of the working class, fear of the casual residuum played a significant part in provoking an intellectual assault which began to be mounted against 'laissez faire' both from right and left in the 1880s (Stedman-Jones, 1971).

Social and educational progress, as ever, owed more to the pressures of national emergency and social anxiety than to the dedication of reformers and the worth of their ideas. What the reformers did — then as now — was to take advantage of the changes made possible by other forces.

It is against this background of new ideas and impending change that we look at educational provision for young children in the nineteenth century

Dame schools and the care of the young
For working mothers with no relatives available to care for their young children, and who were unwilling to leave them unattended at home, the dame school provided a place of safety for their children. Dame schools had long existed, but the numbers increased greatly during the first part of the nineteenth century. The Hadow Report (1933) quotes a Parliamentary estimate of the numbers in 1819 as being 3,102, containing an aggregate of 53,624 pupils, mainly between two and seven years of age. According to this estimate the average size of dame schools was 17, but there must have been considerable variations. The 1851 Census of Education reported that 20 per cent of three year olds and 40 per cent of four year olds were attending schools as 'day' scholars, a total of over a quarter of a million children. Just under a third of the 45,000 schools covered in the Census were classed as 'inferior private schools' (though all 'private' schools, being on average far smaller than 'public' ones,

actually accounted for only a third of all scholars); most of these 'inferior' schools were dame schools providing, according to the Census notes, instruction in reading and, in some cases, writing. The Census report stresses that in looking at the 'inferior' schools, it must not be forgotten that a large proportion of the scholars were children under five.

The decreasing proportion of mothers in employment and the growth in the numbers of children under five in elementary schools must have reduced the demand for child minders and dame schools in the latter half of the century — though they revived in another form in the twentieth century, when younger children were again excluded from the primary schools. (Today their counterparts exist in a few small private nurseries, and in that section of the child-minding service which herds too many young children into dingy basements and kitchens.)

As the Hadow Report points out, the traditional dame schools were, in a sense, infant schools. They served as public nurseries for very young children, being places of security as well (sometimes) as schools; they kept the children of the poor off the streets in towns, and out of the roads and fields in the country. Some dame schools, especially in the villages, were said to be fairly efficient and to undertake some teaching. But the teachers were very often

elderly or invalid women, who were frequently very ignorant. The rooms in which these schools were held were, in many instances, ill-ventilated, ill-kept and unhygienic, [and as late as 1871 the comment was made that dame schools really existed] only to take charge of children while their parents were at work. The fees received by these 'Dames' amounted to 3d or even 4d a week for each child, and the business was a source of profit to persons who could earn a living in no other way.

Though the existence of the dame schools system was said to be in large measure responsible for the slow growth in the development of regular infant schooling for young children, it would be more correct to regard the dame school as an inferior form of nursery centre which parents ceased to use when they were offered something better.

51

Nursery-infant schooling up to 1914

The first real nursery *school* for young children was opened
in 1816 by Robert Owen at the New Lanark cotton mill in
Scotland. Children were admitted from a very young age,
probably from the time they could walk and say a few words,
and were cared for and educated while their parents were at
work in the mill. The school was divided into two classes:
'infant' classes took the children up to the age of about six or
seven; they then passed to the 'superior' school where they
were taught to read, write and count, and the girls to sew,
before starting work themselves in the mill at the age of ten.

Owen believed that man's character was formed by his
environment; he himself loved children and was loved by them;
and he was the kindest and most generous of men. The school
he created admirably expressed his beliefs and character — it
was a model of kindliness, good sense and child-centred
cheerfulness. Owen instructed his teachers:

> they were on no account ever to beat any of the children
> or to threaten them in any manner of word or action, or
> to use abusive terms; but were always to speak to them
> with a pleasant countenance, and in a kind manner and
> tone of voice. That they should tell infants and children
> (for they had all from one to six years old under their
> charge) that they must on all occasions do all that they
> could to make their playfellows happy . . . The school-
> room . . . was furnished with paintings, chiefly of animals,
> with mats, and often supplied with natural objects from
> the garden, fields and woods, the examination and expla-
> nation of which always excited their curiosity and created
> an animated conversation between the children and their
> instructors.

Whitbread (1972) summarises the curriculum that was
followed: singing, dancing, marching to music, fife playing and
geography featured in this infants school curriculum from
which books were excluded, and the children spent three
hours in the open playground. In effect, it was a combined
nursery-infant school, but later the four to six year olds
were given a separate room from the two to four year olds.
At six or seven, children moved into the schoolroom.

Owen's educational methods were based on his intuitive understanding of, and sympathy with, the characteristics of young children. Even his detractors admitted that his school was an outstanding success, and it rapidly became famous: it is said that in ten years nearly 20,000 persons visited it. His educational experiment led to a burst of interest and activity in early education.

The best elements of Owen's system — like that of the Swiss educator Pestalozzi (1745-1827) and, somewhat later, Froebel (1782-1852) — arose out of his concern with the interests and capacities of young children. He postponed formal teaching until the children were aged six or seven because he thought them too young to assimilate formal instruction, and because they distracted older children from paying attention. He devised an interest-centred curriculum which combined group and individual activity and did not force children to do things whose social purpose could not be made intelligible to them. He fed the children properly, encouraged outdoor play, and allowed the young ones to sleep when they were tired. And though the children were 'not to be annoyed with books' (what books *were* there in 1816 suitable for children of so young an age?) they were, in Owen's words, 'taught uses and nature or qualities of the common things around them, by familiar conversation when the child's curiosity was excited so as to induce them to ask questions respecting them. . . . With these infants everything was to be amusement' (cited Blackstone, 1971).

All that we know of Owen, himself a self-educated man whose ideas owed little to his predecessors, stamps him as one of the great educators of all time. Unfortunately most later educators attempted to start formal rote teaching at a much younger age, partly because they equated the education of children with the training of horses, partly because the children left school so young that it was thought necessary to pack as much into their brief years of schooling as possible. In only one respect were the ideas pioneered by Owen consistently adhered to: wherever possible children under the age of seven were taught in separate classes from older children.

One reason why Owen fell into disfavour was that he was a socialist and an atheist. He regarded religion as the chief source of human ills. His uncompromising atheism and his revolutionary activities greatly lessened his popularity in respectable circles, and a much more influential figure in promoting nursery education was Samuel Wilderspin (1792-1856), a sanctimonious pedagogue who, after two years as a teacher in a nursery establishment modelled on Owenite lines in Spitalfield, became a missionary touring the land to preach the gospel of early education. Between 1824 and 1834, largely owing to Wilderspin's efforts, 150 infant schools were started: in Manchester for example there were five, with 743 children on the roll, and in Salford three (Whitbread, 1972).

Wilderspin not only toured widely but wrote several manuals on infant training; his influence was immense. Unfortunately for nursery education and for the children who endured it, Wilderspin's main contributions to educational practice were to popularise mass methods of teaching. His most noteworthy achievement was to invent the tiered gallery. All over the country infant schools were constructed with tiered galleries on which classes of 60 to 100 young children sat in serried rows, on benches, the teacher standing in front of the class, demonstrating, lecturing, hectoring, questioning and teaching by rote.

The galleries were not just a passing fad: they remained a feature of many infant schools until the end of the century. Thus in 1871 the Rules to be Observed in Planning and Fitting Schools, issued by the (governmental) Committee of the Council on Education, stipulated that 'no infant gallery should hold more than 80 or 90 infants'; and in 1885 a rider was added that if more than 80 infants were admitted, one gallery should be provided which should be 'well lighted from one side' (cited Consultative Committee on Infant and Nursery Schools, 1933). So the earliest kind of school building usually had one large oblong shaped schoolroom, its windows about six feet from the floor. The floor itself

inclined slightly from the master's desk to the opposite end of the room, or ended in a gallery. The design was usually ecclesiastical in character, of a type reminiscent of Gothic revival, with stone-mullioned or iron-framed windows glazed with diamond-shaped panes. Even as late as 1870 the ordinary school buildings had not evolved beyond a simple type which consisted of the main school-room sufficiently large to accommodate nearly all the pupils, together with one or possibly two classrooms, provided in most instances with a gallery.

In the early 1900s, a typical infant classroom was still fitted with a fixed tiered gallery in which 50 to 60 or more infants sat in rigid rows. The curriculum consisted largely of the three Rs taught by mechanical drill and rote learning. The children were obliged to write with their right hands, the left being firmly folded behind their backs. Letter cards were used for word building, handwork was carried out by the routine method of teaching the whole class to fold paper, stitch, assemble wooden cubes or lay out sticks in number patterns, and 'object lessons' often became merely 'exercises in stereotyped questions and rote answers from the teacher's manual'. Some drawing and crayoning was undertaken, the children having to copy pictures as accurately as possible. 'Drill and marching, sometimes to martial music, took place in the playground or central hall (Whitbread, 1972).

About this time the galleries were beginning to be removed from the babies' rooms which were being equipped with movable kindergarten desks. In the more progressive schools toys were made available — wooden toys on wheels, hoops, skipping ropes, dolls and dolls' houses, drums or a rocking horse. 'Where there were large numbers of two and three year olds, some were penned in fixed seats with desks along the walls while others used the space in the middle for free activities. Much time was invariably spent on formal class instruction in which the pupils were given an early grounding in the three Rs.'

Though every educational writer from the time of Owen stressed the need to allow young children to spend periods out of doors with the opportunity to engage in 'healthful exercise', as late as 1926 the Code of Regulations for Public Elementary Schools stipulated that 'the recreation period for classes in which the majority of children are under five years of age must be fifteen minutes and may be extended to half an hour, and for other classes must be ten minutes.

Further recreation must not be reckoned as part of the secular instruction.'

The bleakness of infant education

As these facts indicate, the picture of elementary education for young children, especially before the first world war, is a bleak one. The informality, gaiety and spontaneity of the early Owenite schools was replaced by the infant 'system' — rigid, humourless and dreary. It is likely that from the 1860s onwards the quality of education deteriorated, though the supply of places increased rapidly. One factor that was in part responsible for the decline in quality was the infamous Revised|Code of 1862, which, for pupils over the age of six, introduced the deplorable system of payment by results. The Revised Code followed the Report of the Royal Commission under the chairmanship of the Duke of Newcastle set up to inquire into the state of public education in England and to consider and report what measures, if any, were required for the extension of sound and cheap elementary education to all classes of the people. The Newcastle Commission itself expressed strong approval of the value of infant schools and recommended that more training colleges should be established for infant school mistresses. However, the Exchequer grant fixed for payment to local education authorities was only six shillings and sixpence a head as compared with twelve shillings for older children, and inspectors were required to ensure that the attendance of younger pupils did not interfere with the teaching of older ones.

Under the Revised Code payment of the Exchequer grant to local education authorities to keep their schools running was, in the case of younger pupils, based on the average attendance throughout the year. All children over the age of six had, however, to be individually examined each year in the three Rs, and only those who passed the examinations were able to be counted for the purposes of the grant. There was in consequence immense pressure on the schools to drill their pupils in three-R work, for without high pass rates they could not continue financially. All other educational activities were sacrificed to this end, on the erroneous assumption that only by spending more and more time on these dreary exercises would success be achieved.

This iniquitous system continued for thirty years. While it lasted, and for a long time after, it had a backlash effect upon nursery-infant education: teachers in the baby classes had to prepare their children for entry into Standard I, in which they were required to be individually examined. The obvious way to do this seemed to be through pre-reading, pre-writing, pre-arithmetic drill. Thus the formal tests given to older children exerted their influence on the curriculum for younger ones, just as the 11+ examination in primary schools after the second world war caused many teachers of children in the lower classes of the primary schools to begin to prepare their children for the time when they too would have to undergo this ordeal.

The Revised Code, the preposterous architecture of class-rooms, the small playgrounds in the cramped inner city schools, the huge size of classes, the formal teaching, strict discipline and heavy emphasis on religious instruction, and the use of young, unqualified teachers, supervised by head teachers who were often themselves inadequately qualified and insensitive to the needs of children, all contributed to the low quality of early education that was common in the second half of the century. The inadequacy of conditions was recognised by contemporaries, and not least by the government. In its 1904/5 Report, the Board of Education, in discussing the criticisms of early schooling in the 1905 Report of the Board's Women Inspectors acknowledged that

these are criticisms of methods too often employed in Infant Schools [rather] than of the policy of attempting to educate [three and four year old] children. But it must be remembered that the conditions governing size of classes and staffing make it scarcely possible to avoid this type of stricture.

Though standards were generally poor, the quantity of provision for the schooling of children between two and five increased enormously in the second half of the century. Between 1855 and 1870, the proportion of all children attending state-aided schools in Britain made up by three

57

and four year olds doubled from 7.6 per cent to 14.6 per cent. By 1870/1, the proportion of children in this age group in elementary schools was 24.2 per cent. By 1880 it had increased to 29.3 per cent; by 1890 to 33.2 per cent and in 1900 to 43.1 per cent. By the early years of this century, England seemed well on the way to providing a voluntary but freely available educational service for all young children from the age of three if the parents chose to avail themselves of it; and the main need appeared to be the improvement of the quality. Unfortunately, it was just this concern with the quality of education that brought about the collapse of the system. But before we discuss the decline in the services provided for ordinary children of working-class origin the upbringing and education of young middle-class children should first be considered.

Traditional middle-class child care: the British nanny
It was not until after the second world war that the middle and upper classes took much interest in the State system of early education. Before that time they provided for their young children either through the kindergarten movement or, more commonly, through the employment of working-class women to care for them. 'By the end of the nineteenth century you were barely considered middle class if you did not have a nursemaid for your children' (Gathorne-Hardy, 1972). The middle class, in short, relied on a system of minders employed in their own homes, a secure base from which to express criticism of working-class mothers in employment, or advise that the best training for children was that gained from their own mothers in their homes.

Today the nanny is relatively uncommon, at least in her traditional form, though the number of middle-class children cared for in their own homes by *au pairs* and other minders must be considerable. But from 1800, when the habit started to grow considerably, to the second world war, which led to a rapid decline, the employment of nurses or nannies was very common, many middle and upper-class parents seeing their children for no more than an hour, sometimes possibly two, each day For the rest of the time, the children's upbringing was left to nannies and their underlings, the nursery-maids, who wielded their awesome power behind the closed doors of the nursery, far away from parental interference. The numbers involved, according to the historian of the nanny, are startling, and show that the phenomenon cannot be dismissed as interesting but insignificant. At their peak period of use, he estimates, 'we are dealing with something like half a million nannies, at the least perhaps 250,000', and even by 1939 there were at least 144,000, probably between 250,000 and 350,000 (Gathorne-Hardy, 1972).

Nannies could be excellent substitute mothers, greatly loved and fondly remembered in adulthood by their charges. But the system was much open to abuse. Since about a fifth of nannies would move post each year, the children were potentially liable to several changes of primary care-takers in their early years, and these changes, bad enough in themselves, were often handled with great insensitivity to feeling. Many nannies, if not actually cruel (and some were), displayed great harshness, excessive discipline and insistence on routine, general rigidity and discouragement of pleasure and creativity — all this with parents in many cases being unable to exercise adequate supervision, or perhaps not wanting to do so.

The significance of the nanny system is that it demonstrates very clearly how provision for the young reflects the social, economic and ideological realities of the day. The nanny system developed because of great disparities and concentrations of wealth; the surplus of women in the population; a strong belief in hierarchy and a particular sort of 'social order'; and a particular concept of the nature and needs of childhood. The system declined for the same reasons as led to the decline in the numbers of other household servants: fewer single women and full employment, with the possibilities it offered of higher wages for work which did not entail the pettifogging servitude of domestic employment. The demise of the nanny, however, posed for the middle-class mother with young children some of the problems which the working-class mother had faced for a century and a half. This led very many more of them to interest themselves in nursery schools and the playgroup movement — an involvement which has helped to make the expansion of pre-school services highly expedient politically.

There had however been a section of the middle classes who, from the 1850s, had sought early education for their own children outside their homes, in nursery schools or kindergartens, organised on Froebel lines. The motive in this case was educational not philanthropic or expedient (Blackstone, 1971). Whereas nursery education for working-class children was provided largely in response to a manifest need, in the case of middle-class children the service largely preceded the discovery of the need, and was, in large measure, responsible for creating it: the new educational theory of Froebel 'pointed to problems which had previously received little consideration. How might the young child's social and educational development be enhanced?'

Froebel's ideas were virtually unknown in England before 1851 when they were introduced by two German ladies who set up a kindergarten in Bloomsbury. The kindergarten movement developed rapidly after 1870, and in 1871 the first London School Board included in its regulations for infant schools a provision that instruction should be given in object lessons of a simple character with such exercises of the hands and eyes as were given in the kindergarten system. Two years later the London School Board appointed an instructor in kindergarten exercises who began giving classes for teachers. In 1888 the National Froebel Union was founded as an examining body.

The essence of Froebel's teaching was well summarised by a Report made by one of HM Inspectors in 1854. The system, he said, 'treats the child as a child; encourages it to think for itself; teaches it by childish toys and methods gradually to develop in action or hieroglyphic writing its own ideas, to state its own story, and to listen to that of others . . . . the grand feature of the system is "occupation". The child is taught little; it simply produces for itself' (cited Consultative Committee on Infant and Nursery Schools, 1933).

Froebel's most enduring contribution to nursery education lay in the importance which he ascribed to play, which he regarded as the *work* of the child. His pedagogy was explicitly developmental, in that the role of the teacher became that of assisting the child to realise his potentialities at the time; and the good teacher, like the good gardener, merely provided the conditions for optimal growth. As would be expected from someone starting with these philosophical premises, Froebel provided little in the way of a set curriculum for children. He did however devise a series of 'occupations' — handwork exercises graded in difficulty which were said to 'cover the whole field of intuitive and sensory instruction and lay the basis for all further teaching'. In many elementary schools these were widely used by teachers who found the spirit of Froebel's system incomprehensible, but who taught the children his 'occupations' in a manner as stereotyped and formal as the rest of the curriculum they imposed on them. The result was a travesty of all that Froebel stood for, and was vigorously condemned over and over again by inspectors and educational reformers.

Though the number of Froebel kindergartens remained small, Froebel's influence continued to grow. The kindergarten showed by comparison how poor was the quality of the education in the elementary school; and both educators and school doctors expressed increasing concern at the possibility that very young children might actually be harmed by going to school. The Report of the Inter-Departmental Committee on Physical Deterioration (1904) had called attention to the unhygienic conditions in public elementary schools and recommended that systematic medical inspection of all school children should be imposed as a public duty on every local education authority; and the same year the Board of Education decided to employ six of the recently appointed Women Inspectors to conduct an inquiry regarding the admission of infants to public elementary schools and the curriculum suitable for children under the age of five. Their Report was published in 1905, and triggered off profound changes.

The decline of nursery-infant education

As we have seen, between 1871 and 1900 the proportion of children aged three to four in school rose from 24.2 per cent to 43.1 per cent of the age group. By 1910 the percentage had fallen to 22.7 per cent, by 1920 to 15.3 per cent and by 1931 to 13.1 per cent. The rise in numbers up to 1900 coincided with a fall in the numbers of mothers in paid employment and so cannot be explained by a growing need for day care, though undoubtedly for some it served this purpose. The most important factor must rather have been the increasing availability of provision. The 1870 Education Act gave parents a right of admission for their children under five, though compulsory school did not start till five. In 1891, schooling was made free and the last barrier for the children of the poorly paid and unemployed was removed. In 1905, however, education authorities were given discretionary powers to withdraw this right of admission for under-fives for any school maintained by them, and after this date, numbers, which had begun to decrease slowly after 1901, began to fall very rapidly as authorities cut back provision for the age group. By 1908 the Consultative Committee on the School Attendance of Children Under Five, found that more than half of the 322 education authorities replying to their inquiry had applied these powers, at least to some schools or in some areas, and the Committee observed that 'it is evident that many authorities have based [their] actions . . . from the point of view of finance or have treated them in an uncertain manner without the serious consideration [the matter] deserves.'

The decline in three and four year olds attending schools reflected the official policy of education authorities rather than changing parental demand. The Board of Education Reports on early schooling in the 1900s give us some insight into the reasons for this demand. One Woman Inspector in the 1905 Report lists the reasons given by the Attendance Officers in Cardiff for children being sent to school at three — a popular head teacher or babies' teacher; because custom and the law permitted; convenience for the mothers, leaving those in better-off districts free to go out and in poorer districts to spend time in gossip or drinking (though whether tea or something stronger is not clear); to avoid the need for older children to be kept at home looking after younger brothers and sisters; and because poverty compelled many mothers to send children to school while they worked.

Another Woman Inspector reporting on the situation in London, believed attitudes to early schooling varied according to class:

[better-class] mothers voiced complaints about many aspects of existing provision (e.g. with regard to moral effects there is no doubt that many of the best mothers are greatly dissatisfied . . . find children coming home dirty in body and irreverant in language and habits) . . . [for poorer mothers by comparison] the school and staff were often a comfort and delight . . . they are surprised and delighted with their offsprings' progress and their chief wish is that school doors never close for holidays . . . among the poorer class there is an increasing desire to send their children as early as the authorities will take them (Board of Education, 1905).

A rather more extensive exercise, mounted by the Consultative Committee using NSPCC Inspectors, and covering 479 homes, gave a somewhat different picture: 384 were in favour of early school attendance. Among the reasons for this view were — children are kept warm, clean, safe; keeps them off the streets and from learning bad habits; they learn good manners and obedience; keeps them out of the way; allows mother to work; the children are happier and cannot get into mischief; they learn a little. No division of views was found between 'better' and 'worse' classes of parents, many 'careful' parents keeping children at home, while others equally 'careful' sent them to school (Board of Education, 1908). The survey leaves the impression that parental attitudes to early schooling in the 1900s were not dissimilar to those of today. It will be noted that educational reasons for school attendance (if by that we mean 'learns a little') came very far down in the list.

The decline in numbers during the first half of the twentieth century was in part brought about through the competing claims of other parts of the state school system, for money and resources at a time when increasing numbers of children of compulsory school age had to be provided for. But the position of the under-fives was also being undermined by increasing objections in principle to schooling for this age group.

It was to make a systematic investigation of this charge that the six Women Inspectors of the Board of Education carried out their inquiry in 1904. The Report published in 1905, was unequivocal in its condemnation: the Inspectors were agreed that children between the ages of three and five 'gained no profit intellectually from school instruction, and that the mechanical teaching which they so often received dulled their imagination and weakened their power of independent observation.' Children under five would, they argued, be better out of schools altogether. Those who came from good homes ought to remain at home with their mothers. For those who were not so fortunate — and these included substantial numbers of slum children — a new type of provision of 'nursery schools rather than schools of instruction' should be set up. But there was no clear idea of what form these should take, and the Board was asked to consider the question further.

In 1907 the Board of Education gave their Consultative Committee a reference to follow up the Inspectors' Report. Its terms contained more than a hint of what the Board had in mind:

> To consider and advise the Board of Education in regard to the desirability, or otherwise, both on educational and other grounds, of discouraging the attendance at school of children under the age of (say) five years, on the assumption that, in the event of the change being found generally desirable, the moneys now payable by the Board of Education in the shape of grants in respect of the attendance of such children, should still be payable to Local Education Authorities, in greater relief of their expenditure in educating children over five years of age.

The Report was published in 1908. The Committee agreed that the Inspectors had been right in their claim that much of what was taught young children in elementary schools was worse than useless. However, they added, the 1905 Report had been open to misinterpretation over its conclusion that three to five year olds gained practically no intellectual advantage from any school instruction:

> . . . so far as this means that (these) children get no intellectual advantage from formal instruction and discipline, it

is no doubt a fair summary of the [Women Inspectors']
views. But it is at least liable to be taken as referring to any
form of school instruction and has been so taken, though
in our opinion this goes a good deal beyond the reports
themselves.

In general, the Committee argued that the whole question of
school attendance for younger children was greatly confused
by a failure to distinguish old fashioned institutions with
formal instruction and discipline from schools where the
special needs of small children were met. 'Many objections
urged against the attendance of younger children at school
are made on the assumption that all schools are old fashioned
and not likely to be improved to any great extent . . . this
is not the case.'
The Committee came down firmly in favour of nursery
schooling where the need existed. Towards nursery education
it adopted a pragmatic and compassionate approach that is
still impressive:

the Committee are of the opinion that the best training
for children between three and five is that which they get
from their mothers in their own homes, providing there
exist adequate opportunities for the necessary maternal
care and training . . . at present such homes are not always
found . . . not only [because] parents are not sufficiently
alive to the well-being of their children [but also because]
many mothers are unable to train them at home due to
various circumstances [i.e. because they] lack the necessary
means or accommodation [or because they] may be
compelled to work. The Committee think that it is
necessary that some public authority should provide
opportunities for suitable training and education of great
numbers of little children . . . and in the greater part of
most towns and urban areas [this will mean] the majority
of children. . . . The condition of English working-class life
must be taken as it is found. It is fatal to ignore this and
insist prematurely on a general adoption of a system which,
however desirable in theory, is limited to those parts of the
community where industrial and social conditions are
in an unusually advanced state. For the present, the

Committee consider that nursery schools are in many cases a practical necessity.

The Committee's conclusion in favour of nursery schools, and even its 'detailed and enlightened guidance on premises, equipment, curriculum and staffing' of these schools, did nothing to stop the slide in the numbers of under-fives in the state education system. For though the reports of the 1900s had upheld the principle of early education (albeit with an initial assumption that home life was preferable where good standards could be attained), much of the existing early educational provision was manifestly unsatisfactory and an improved system, possibly based on nursery schooling was needed to replace it. But a reluctance to spend extra money; education authorities struggling to cope with compulsory education and expand schooling for older children; widespread objections to the very idea of early education; and no strong lobbies for its improvement (the middle class had little interest as yet in the state educational system) — all these meant that a decline in numbers rather than a campaign to improve and expand the service was the inevitable outcome.

Conclusions

In looking at the nineteenth century it is clear that attitudes towards children, and services for them, are influenced by prevailing ideas about the significance and needs of childhood. But how relevant is what happened then to the problems we face today?

First, in the growth of class consciousness and increasing differences in class experiences, behaviour and attitudes during the last century, lie the roots of many of today's class-related differences in child-rearing behaviour.

Secondly, the failure to sustain the growth and improve the quality of early education ensured that the extension of pre-school education would be left as a major issue for the present day. The opportunity in the 1900s to build on the increasingly well-established pattern of early schooling and combine this with the fund of knowledge and ideas on nursery schooling then becoming available, was wasted. Not only could initiatives taken then have given the country an early and sound foundation of nursery education, they might also have made it possible to avoid the present fragmentation of education and day-care services for the under fives.

Educational developments in the period under consideration also left their mark on present-day organisation of services. The establishment of the compulsory school age at five, the withdrawal of the right to education for three and four year olds and the assumption of the reports of the 1900s that the education of young children should occur in separate nursery schools, a response to the discrediting of provision in elementary schools, all played their part in ensuring that the basic unit of early compulsory education would become five to eleven, rather than two or three to seven or eight. 'Pre-school' became defined as under five and even the present-day emphasis on admitting 'rising fives' to primary schools and adding nursery classes to them, implies a tacking-on of these young children to the basic 5+ unit.

Thirdly, the history of early childhood in the nineteenth century was played out against a background of increasing physical separation of work, leisure, home-making and child-rearing, as increasing numbers of men and women left domestic industry for the factory and as the school, friendly society, club and other organisations for leisure and instruction played a growing part in working-class life. It is of course dangerous to over-generalise the scope of this movement. Many workers in such industries as mining, transport and agriculture had always had to work outside the home.

Overall, what did occur in the century was an increasing segregation of functions together with increasingly narrowly defined roles for children, men and women. Faced by a growing distaste for married women going out to work, and a decreasing need for them in the work force, wives and mothers found their roles increasingly restricted to housework and child-rearing, and their lives more and more cut off from contact with other work and social activities. The world of children was also becoming segregated from such non-domestic activities and from the world of men. The view that teaching and other work with young children was an exclusively female preserve had taken firm root by the end of the century. By this time, too, only a minority of adults could look back to a

67

childhood in the more integrated community of the village or to the experience of growing up in a family whose members worked together in domestic industry. Fewer still would have been introduced to the world of domestic work before five, though for their parents and grandparents, experience of early work was more common.

People living in the last century faced an enormous task in coming to terms with the Industrial Revolution and its consequences, a task which required the development of methods of social statistics and research and an increase in knowledge in the fields of health, education and social administration. Not only were they ill-equipped to grasp the nature of the problems they faced and formulate effective answers to them, but they were also faced with a population which was increasing at a very rapid rate.

Obviously in the present century standards of life and services have greatly improved for children under five — mortality rates are an indicator of the improvement made — but much of this is due to generally rising standards of material prosperity and to the development of services which the Victorians were groping their way towards. For they, struggling to come to terms with the whole question of state intervention in mass, compulsory education, were able to offer schooling of a sort to nearly half their three to four year olds. That over three-quarters of this century will have passed before we regain this level of provision is an indication of how smug we can afford to be in looking back at the Victorians.

The decline in the numbers of under fives in schools which
had begun at the beginning of the twentieth century was very
rapid. By 1904 there were practically no children under three
in elementary schools and by 1911 the number of three and
four year olds had nearly halved. By 1930 the proportion of
three and four year olds at elementary schools had dropped to
13 per cent from 43 per cent in 1900 (Consultative Committee
on Infant and Nursery Schools, 1933). Nor did separate
nursery schools increase in number to any appreciable
extent, though government policy had been to encourage
them — without however providing funds or pressure to do
so.

By the beginning of the twentieth century voluntary day
nurseries were beginning to expand and organise, and in 1906
the National Society of Day Nurseries was founded, representing some thirty day nurseries. However the first major expansion came after the outbreak of the first world war. Women
were needed to work in the munitions factories and so
nurseries to look after their children were publicly provided
through grants from the Board of Education. By 1919, 174
such nurseries existed (Ferguson and Fitzgerald, 1954).

A distinction between a child's health and physical
requirements and his educational and social needs had unfortunately been made by the end of the first world war and
these two aspects had become the interest of two quite
separate groups of people — the medical and nursing profes-
sion and the educationalists. The 1918 Education Act
empowered local education authorities to establish nursery
schools or classes and aid voluntary schools, and the 1918
Maternity and Child Welfare Act empowered local welfare
authorities to set up day nurseries and to grant-aid voluntary
nurseries.

69

Unfortunately again, lack of public financial backing and the stringencies of the interwar period limited development in both fields. In spite of this the pressure to provide more continued, and even during the years of the great economic depression things looked promising.

In 1933 an enormous boost was given to the development of nursery education by the report of the Consultative Committee on Infant and Nursery Schools, under the chairmanship of Sir W.H. Hadow. Whilst the best place for a child under five was thought to be at home with his mother, it was recognised that where the mother worked, and where home conditions were unsatisfactory, nursery education in separate nursery schools or classes should be provided. Emphasis was laid on physical wellbeing and development, but mental and intellectual development, and the influence of early experiences, were also considered important. 'What is true of education at every period of child life is true most of all during the nursery period; its aim is not so much to impart the knowledge and the habits which civilised adults consider useful, as to aid and supplement the natural growth of the normal child.' We may rightly regard the function of the nursery school or class as educational, but we must not regard it as didactic. The aim of the teacher will be primarily to assist the spontaneous unfolding of the child's natural powers . . . The nursery school must accordingly endeavour so far as is possible to plant the child in his natural biological environment, to keep him out of doors with plenty of air, sunlight and space, surrounded with trees, plants and animals, with places that he can explore, pools where he can paddle and sandpits where he can dig (Consultative Committee on Infant and Nursery Schools, 1933).

For three years nothing happened, but in 1936 local education authorities started planning their expansion in nursery education. By 1938 there were 118 nursery schools and 104 day nurseries. The following year the second world war broke out.

The upheaval in family life brought an early realisation that existing forms of service and provision for mothers and young families were very inadequate. New strategies were adopted and changed to deal with new situations as they arose and by

70

the end of the war a great variety of systems and services existed.

The second world war

The first problem was caused by the evacuation of large numbers of mothers with children under five. Settling into someone else's home with no work to do and no school for the young children to go to imposed great strains both on evacuees and on the host community. So the Nursery Centres Scheme was evolved by the Ministry of Health and Board of Education. Centres staffed by voluntary workers under a trained teacher were to be set up where the children could play, and learn social behaviour. These became a reality in 1940 with Treasury funds and the second wave of evacuation.

In the early years of the war day nurseries had largely been set up at the initiative of individual local authorities according to their priorities and local circumstances. In 1940 Treasury money was made available for new nurseries in areas where the Ministry of Labour reported an actual and potential shortage of women workers: these were set up under the responsibility of the local Medical Officer of Health and in the control of a matron. Response was however sporadic, as it had been to the National Minders Scheme — an expedient by the Ministry of Labour to combat the slow growth of day nurseries. Volunteer minders, paid jointly by the Ministry of Health and the mothers, were asked to register with the maternity and child welfare authorities.

By this time, employment problems were developing. In some areas such as London it happened earlier, but in 1941 a general need was evident for women to work in industry — and also in order to supplement their husband's meagre Service pay; and the Ministry of Labour was particularly concerned about the state of existing provision for the care of pre-school children. The confusion caused by the coexistence of nursery schools, nursery classes, day nurseries and the Nursery Centres Scheme, as well as the voluntarily run play schemes and creches, split between two different ministries, led to a great desire for some coordination.

The entrenched positions of those who favoured providing day care for young children in day nurseries and those who

71

advocated nursery *schooling* made it difficult to agree a national policy. However the special needs of the under twos swung the balance in favour of day nurseries, and local welfare authorities under the Ministry of Health became responsible for setting up wartime nurseries. An informal committee of voluntary agencies was established, the Board of Education creating a division on Care of the Under fives to advise the Ministry of Health on the education side of day nurseries. The Ministry of Labour advised where nurseries should be set up.

The nurseries were to be open twelve to fifteen hours a day and mothers in employment were to be charged a fee; a nursery school teacher was to supervise the older children. Expansion was rapid; from 194 nurseries (in England and Wales) in 1941 to 1,450 whole time nurseries taking 68,181 children in 1944 with another 109 part-time nurseries with 3,625 children. (By contrast, in 1974 there were 517 day nurseries taking children, though the numbers of mothers of young children in full-time employment was much larger in 1974 than in 1944). In addition there were 35,000 children in nursery schools and classes and another 103,000 children in reception classes in elementary schools (Ferguson and Fitzgerald, 1954).

After the war, the coordination of Health, Education and Labour Ministries in the care of under fives broke. The need for both day nurseries and nursery schools was recognised but the division between them was embodied in law.

The post-war period

The 1944 Education Act reaffirmed the minimum compulsory school age as five years and laid upon local education authorities the duty of providing full-time education from that age. In fulfilling this duty, however, education authorities were to 'have regard to the need for securing that provision is made for pupils who have not attained the age of five years by the provision of nursery schools or, where the authority consider the provision of such schools to be inexpedient, by the provision of nursery classes in other schools.' No charge was to be made to parents whose children attended these educational establishments — the principle that education should be 'free' was reaffirmed for this as for other forms of schooling.

Two years later, the legislative basis for the provision of day nurseries was laid down in the National Health Service Act, 1946, which stated baldly that

It shall be the duty of every local health authority to make arrangements for the care, including in particular dental care, of expectant and nursing mothers and of children who have not attained the age of five years and are not attending primary schools maintained by a local education authority.

The Act also empowered local authorities to make charges according to means for these services. However, even in 1945, the Ministry of Health had made it quite clear that it disapproved of care in day nurseries unless circumstances were exceptional. It is worth quoting from this circular as it is one of the earliest government statements to show the attitudes shaping the recent development of pre-school provision in Britain. The circular (Ministry of Health circular 221/45) said:

The Ministers concerned accept the view of medical and other authority that, in the interest of the health and development of the child no less than for the benefit of the mother, the proper place for a child under two is at home with his mother. They are also of the opinion that, under normal peacetime conditions, the right policy to pursue would be positively to discourage mothers of children under two from going out to work; to make provision for children between two and five by way of nursery schools and nursery classes; and to regard day nurseries and daily guardians as supplements to meet the special needs (where these exist and cannot be met within the hours, age, range and organisation of nursery school and nursery classes) of children whose mothers are constrained by individual circumstances to go out to work or whose home conditions are in themselves unsatisfactory from the health point of view, or whose mothers are incapable for some good reason of undertaking the full care of their children.

The assumptions and beliefs which lie behind this statement

73

have guided the subsequent development of pre-school provision, and can be seen in different guises up to the present. It is accepted that there is a body of professional authority which knows the best way to bring up young children, and the form that services to meet their needs should take; care by anyone other than the mother is harmful under the age of two, or for more than a certain time between the ages of two and five; day care outside the home is necessary or beneficial under certain circumstances (needs of the country, financial necessity, bad housing, personal inadequacy); nursery schooling is beneficial for everyone.

The immediate post-war years

In 1945, because of the wartime expansion of day nurseries for working women, there were 1,300 nurseries (England and Wales) but only 75 nursery schools. According to government policy, however, nursery schools and classes were to be expanded, and day nurseries reduced to the minimum. In 1946, therefore, a considerable number of wartime day nurseries were transferred to local education authorities to be run as nursery schools; by the beginning of 1947 there were 902 day nurseries and 353 nursery schools. At the same time, of all young children who received any form of nursery service, by far the greatest number, some 116,000, were in ordinary classes in primary schools, while another 68,000 were in special nursery classes attached to ordinary primary schools, unlike nursery schools which were separate institutions, not attached to an infant school.

The transfer of responsibility for the great bulk of nursery provision from Health to Education had two consequences that were little appreciated at the time. First, because schools kept short hours and had long holidays, mothers whose work could not be adjusted to fit in with patterns of schooling had to make private arrangements for their children. Secondly, the age at which public provision began to become available, except for the small number of younger children in day nurseries, was raised from two to three — since nursery schools on educational grounds discouraged the admission of younger children.

Unfortunately once again the hoped-for expansion in

74

nursery education did not take place. Although local education authorities submitted plans for a considerable increase in both nursery schools and nursery classes, there was a shortage of building labour and materials, and an increasing school population in the compulsory age-range to accommodate. In consequence, the numbers of nursery classes in primary schools began to fall, and nursery schools increased in number only very slowly. Reports on the progress in nursery education actually disappeared from the pages of the Ministry of Education annual reports until 1964 when the topic reappeared with the explanation that

> since the war it has not been possible to allow local education authorities to extend their provision for children below compulsory school age in nursery schools and classes, mainly because it was felt that worthwhile provision was bound to absorb teachers badly needed in the primary schools.

At the same time, day nursery places were decreasing in line with government policy so the outlook for mothers who wanted their young children looked after in schools or nurseries was dim. Once again, therefore, the private sector began to make up the deficiency.

The 1950s

The 1950s was a period of quiet stagnation in the field of pre-school provision. In 1951 the annual report of the Ministry of Health stated that day nursery places could only be justified 'where children in special need on health or social grounds were concerned', and not where the need 'arose from the mother's desire to supplement the family income by going out to work'. Day nurseries were steadily closed down, and by 1963, 13 county boroughs and 13 counties had closed all their nurseries. The numbers of registered child minders and private nurseries gradually increased but nursery school and nursery class places showed little change during this period. There were no government statements or circulars from either Ministry and annual reports confine themselves to an account of numbers.

One development which was insignificant in terms of numbers during the 1950s, but which involved a very important change in nursery education practice, went unremarked for several years.

This was the introduction of part-time nursery education. It was first recorded in primary schools in 1955 and in nursery schools in 1958, and by 1960 involved only some 3,400 pupils. However, in this year, the Ministry of Education issued a circular (number 8/60) which told local authorities that, for reasons of economy, there could be no expansion of nursery school provision but drew their attention to the shift system whereby two children could occupy one nursery school place by attending for half a day each — a practical solution to give more children nursery schooling without increasing costs. However, by the 1970s, as will be discussed later, the numbers of part-time pupils had increased dramatically, and part-time education for the under fives had become not just a regrettable practical necessity, but a policy justified on educational grounds and a principle for future expansion. Figures 2 and 3 show this trend.

The 1960s: playgroups and child minders

Though the 1960s were years of expansion elsewhere in the education service, the government did very little for young children. Indeed in 1960 a Ministry of Education circular (number 8/60) reaffirmed the government's intention that there should be no further expansion in nursery education. The Ministry of Health and the local health authorities adopted a similar attitude to day care: the number of nurseries did not increase, and the conditions of entry were as restricted as ever. If anything, in fact, they were more so for children of working mothers, since increasingly high priority came to be given to the children of women who were psychiatrically disordered, or single parents, or destitute.

However, public and parental interest in young children's welfare and education was growing. Young mothers who before the war might have had a nursemaid to help them with their children were now doing so on their own. The war had greatly disturbed long-established communities, and the rehousing programme drew parents of young

POST-WAR DEVELOPMENT OF EDUCATION FOR THE UNDER-FIVES (England & Wales)

Figure 2: Pupils under five in maintained primary schools

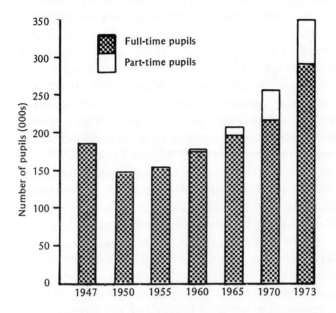

Figure 3: Pupils in maintained nursery schools

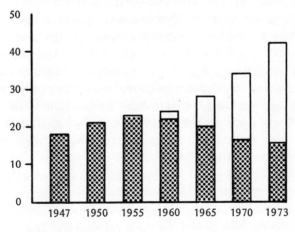

See Tables 2 and 3

children away from the support of their wider family and neighbourhood. The opportunities for young children to play in yards or on the street declined as more families came to live in flats, and as the traffic built up in the residential areas. Families, and especially mothers, came to see their young children's needs both for safe places to play and for the company of other children.

Out of this grew the playgroup movement. Historically it started in New Zealand, but during the 1960s similar movements sprang up in a number of European countries, apparently more or less independently. In Britain the movement began in 1960 when a mother who had organised some neighbours with other young children into a group which met regularly in each others' homes, sharing the tasks of child care, wrote to the *Guardian* encouraging others to do likewise − offering advice. She was swamped with replies (Van der Eyken, 1974) and the Playgroup Movement began.

By 1965 there were 500 groups; ten years later the Pre-school Playgroups Association, the largest coordinating body, had a membership of 9,100 groups (*Guardian*, 17 April 1975). By 1972 the latest date for which official figures are available, the total number of playgroups in England was given as 15,266 (*Hansard*, 24 June 1972).

Today playgroups vary greatly in size and the manner in which they function. The large ones often have trained staff, many of whom will have got their training by attending courses run by the PPA or some other body, though some are trained teachers. Parry and Archer report that the 100 or so playgroups run by the Save the Children Playgroup Society in areas of high need, serve families where parents are not able to take much part in running them. The Society therefore strongly advises the appointment of paid, trained and experienced leaders for each group, to give security and continuity to the children and to guide those parents who help on a rota basis.

During the 1960s private nursery schools also grew rapidly, although the term 'nursery school' can be confusing. Most private nursery schools, which vary a great deal in size, structure and methods, are in fact registered with social service departments as private nurseries, along with playgroups and private day nurseries. The official DHSS statistics do not distinguish between them despite their obvious differences in function and organisation. Only a few (114 in 1973) are recognised and registered with the Department of Education and Science as schools. However we are able to distinguish within the private nursery category those which offer all day care (951 in 1973). These are likely to be fee-paying nurseries rather than playgroups since playgroups rarely take children all day.

The charge is often made that playgroups and private nurseries are essentially middle-class institutions. But as Van der Eyken (1974) points out, *all* pre-school education is in a sense middle-class, 'for it is only the middle classes who can contemplate paying fees to have children in organised groups, or consider taking a child to a nursery at 9 am only to fetch it again at noon, take it back at 1.15 pm and fetch it again at 3.30 pm. Pre-schooling is essentially a middle-class concern, and it is a reflection of our divided society that whereas this aspect has been amenable to voluntary action, there has been no complementary drive to provide all-day care for the growing number of mothers who, through economic necessity, have to leave their children to go out to work. For such a mother, the playgroup is an irrelevance.'

Child minders

Playgroups are no use to working mothers. And as more mothers sought employment more of them turned to child minders as the only way in which they could ensure that their young children were physically looked after while they were at work. How many children came to be looked after in this way we do not know. Brian Jackson, who a few months earlier estimated that 100,000 young children (60,000 of them black) were being illegally child-minded, in 1974 (*Guardian*, July 23), revised his estimate to 330,000. It is a revealing comment on our ignorance that we simply cannot say which of these figures is more nearly correct. Since 1948 child minders have been obliged to register with the local authority if they mind children for profit. The law is however a dead letter, and it is known that most minders are not in fact registered. Consequently the official numbers,

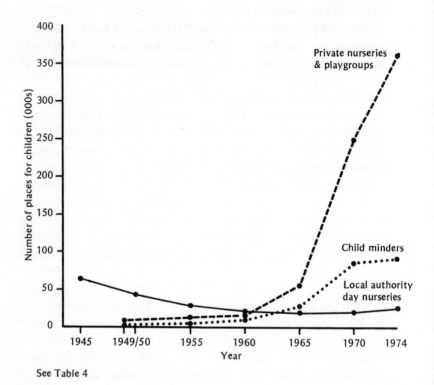

Figure 4: Development of day care facilities (registered with the Department of Health & Social Security) in England & Wales

See Table 4

presented in Figure 4 along with other services associated with local authority social services departments, are misleading rather than informative.

The conditions under which children are looked after by child minders are likewise undocumented. The Child Minding Research Unit set up by Brian and Sonia Jackson to inquire into child minding has published heartrending accounts of individual cases of the grossest neglect, as did Yudkin (1967) in the 1960s. But it is impossible from these to get an overall picture, or to know whether numbers are still increasing, or to compare standards of care today with those of ten years ago. Our ignorance of these matters tells its own story.

The expansion of nursery services

Although an embargo had been placed on the expansion of day nurseries and nursery schools by the Ministry of Health and the Ministry of Education respectively, they each made one exception in the mid 1960s. Money was not available for a general increase of nursery provision, but the country was short of trained teachers, so in 1964 and 1965 addenda to circular 8/60 (which had forbidden further expansion) were issued by the Department of Education and Science

Day care and nursery education in 1966 (England and Wales)

	Number of schools, premises or persons	Number of children	% population 0—4 years
Nursery schools	462	28,461	0.7
Under fives in primary schools (nursery and other classes)	not known	209,211	5.0
Day nurseries (run by local authority)	445	21,157	0.5
Private nurseries (inc. playgroups, nurseries, nursery schools)	3,083	75,132	1.8
Registered child minders	3,887	32,336	0.8
TOTAL		366,297	8.8

Source: see Tables 2, 3 and 4

to allow the provision of nursery school places where this would release married women teachers with young children to go back to work. In 1966 the Ministry of Health made a similar exception for the setting up of day nurseries for the children of nurses who were also in short supply; the official position for the rest of the population was still that day nurseries were only for those mothers in unfortunate circumstances and great need, and not for those who preferred to go to work.

In 1966, the general overall picture for all forms of pre-school provision was as shown in the table on page 81. Only 8.8 per cent of all children under five had access to any of the known forms of provision.

However, the following year, 1967, was to see the beginning of a great public interest in the education and day care of young children. The Plowden Report, the Seebohm Report, the Urban Aid Programme and the Halsey Report, all came out in quick succession, and local authorities were at last permitted to expand their provision for the under fives.

The Plowden Report and the White Paper

In 1963, the Central Council for Education had been asked to 'consider the whole subject of primary education and the transition to secondary education', and a committee under the chairmanship of Lady Plowden was set up to do just this. Its findings (Central Advisory Council for Education 1967) were based on visits to schools and on oral and written evidence from teachers and local authority associations, educational bodies, individuals from the Department of Education and Science, school inspectors and others. In addition, a survey of 173 schools, their teachers and parents, was undertaken.

The Report came to several important conclusions upon which the planned development of nursery education is now based. The gains from nursery education for both parents and children were thought to be great and the principle of nursery education on demand established. There were, however, two important qualifications to this. First, education was in principle to be part-time, as a whole day's separation from mother was regarded as inadvisable; secondly nursery education

82

was not suitable for children under three who should be with their mothers. The Report also introduced the concept of educational priority areas and positive discrimination to offset the educational disadvantage produced by a poor environment. For children in such 'need', nursery schooling was thought to be especially beneficial and for many of them it could with advantage be full-time. However, day nurseries were still considered to be the best form of care for children under three. The Plowden Report did acknowledge that some children would need looking after outside the short nursery school hours it proposed, and very briefly suggested, some combination of services in children's centres or nursery centres. This idea was not expanded and has scarcely been taken up since.

Plowden turned these conclusions into estimates of demand, though on what basis is not clear. The parents of half the number of three year olds were thought to want nursery schooling for their children, and 90 per cent of four year olds. It was estimated that *at least* 15 per cent of the three to four year olds would need full-time provision: this was based on 5 per cent of mothers having to work full time, 10 per cent unable to look after their children, plus an unidentifiable number of single parents, very large families, overcrowded families and sick mothers. The Plowden Committee estimated that its recommendations would require the equivalent of 745,750 nursery places in 1975.

These recommendations were not acted upon by the government until 1972, but an Action Research Project was set up in 1967/8 in four areas of the country to look at practical ways of improving educational opportunities and standards in educational priority areas (Halsey, 1972b). Round about the same time the Urban Aid Programme was set up by the Local Government Grants (Social Need) Act, 1969. This allowed money to be paid from the Treasury to local authorities 'who . . . are required in the exercise of any of their functions to incur expenditure by reason of the existence in any urban area of special social need'. Social need was not defined in the Act, but guidelines were given in subsequent circulars. Broadly it meant multiple deprivation in urban areas distinguished by such characteristics as poor housing, high unemployment, poor schools, large families, high proportions of children in care or in trouble, high levels of immigrants. The Home Office was made responsible for coordinating the programme, which is still in operation. It seeks advice from appropriate government departments in deciding which projects to grant-aid.

In each phase of the Urban Aid Programme circulars were issued to local authorities outlining the sort of projects that would receive priority, and inviting bids for the money available. Nursery education and day nurseries received priority from the beginning, but were phased out as the Department of Health and the Department of Education put their own plans for expansion into effect. In the first nine phases of the Urban Programme from 1968 to 1973, nursery education, day nurseries and playgroups in England and Wales received over £13 million out of the £31 million available (information from the Home Office, unpublished). By 1975 a total of 24,000 nursery school or class places had been created under the Urban Programme (Department of Education and Science, 1975c).

In 1972 a government White Paper on education was published (Department of Education and Science 1972) which announced 'a major initiative in the provision of facilities for the under fives.' The conclusions and estimates given in the Plowden Report were accepted — that most needs could be met by part-time education and that places should be provided for all three and four year olds whose parents wanted them. It was envisaged that expansion would take up to 1982, by which time there should be places available for 50 per cent of all three year olds, and 90 per cent of four year olds, though local authorities were to develop their plans in the light of local conditions. The government believed it right for most of the provisions to be in nursery classes in primary schools, both in order to avoid a change of school at age five and on the grounds of cost.

The White Paper went on to say that 'the majority of educationists regard part-time attendance at school as sufficient, indeed preferable, for most children until they reach compulsory school age', and estimated that only 15 per cent of places were needed for full-time attendance.

Following the White Paper, the Department of Education and Science issued circular 2/73 to local authorities putting these principles into practice. £15 million a year was to be made available for the expansion of nursery education and local authorities were asked to assess their needs and submit them with building project requirements. It was made clear that there would be no central government resources for nursery provision for two year olds.

This completed the process of effectively excluding two year olds, and some three year olds from the state nursery education system. Even though financial restrictions had limited the number of places available for two year olds in school in the early part of the century, the Hadow Report in 1933 had assumed their inclusion in the state education system as had the Ministry of Health in 1945 (in the circular cited earlier in this chapter). Between then and the time Plowden reported in 1968, the scope of nursery education somehow contracted to include only children over three; so that the Department of Education circular (2/73) which put the Plowden Committee's recommendations into effect, only considered admissions to nursery classes the term *after* a child's third birthday. In local education authorities which only have one yearly admission point, this means that some children will not be eligible until they are nearly four.

Day care

While developments in nursery education were taking place, parallel events were happening in the field of day care. Yudkin in 1967 had deplored the lack of any coherent policy about pre-school children and the haphazard services which arose from the multiplicity of departments and agencies separately involved in the field, but still education and day care were looked at quite separately, with some squabbling about playgroups in the middle.

A year after Plowden had reported on primary schools and nursery education, an official committee chaired by Frederic Seebohm published its Report on local authority social services (Committee on Local Authority and Allied Personal Social Services, 1968). One section of the Report was concerned with social services for children: Seebohm pointed out how the historic accident, by which the wartime need for day nurseries was developed in the organisational framework of the maternity and child welfare service and the health department, had been perpetuated and subsequently maintained by legislation. The committee maintained that fragmentation and lack of coordinated policy had had a disastrous effect on services; nonetheless it ultimately approved the status quo in both provision and staff training though it could not agree whether playgroups provided care or education.

Seebohm went on to say that there were not enough places available in day nurseries, that expansion in nursery education would not cater for everyone, and that additional nursery places should be made available not only for children whose mothers were 'unable to be wholly responsible for looking after them' but for other groups as well. Amongst these were isolated mothers, those with large families, and those who undergo the stresses which many families with under fives experience.

One omission in the whole consideration is any comment on the *type* of care children should receive: education is not mentioned as a function of day nurseries, though social care is mentioned as a function of education. Again, despite the obvious benefits which could be seen to accrue from an expansion of day care, Seebohm too was led to maintain that 'it is detrimental to the young child to be separated from its mother for long periods.'

On the heels of Seebohm came circular 37/68 from the Ministry of Health to local authorities, giving approval, within financial constraints, to the expansion of day nursery places. It spelt out quite clearly the circumstances under which children could be offered day nursery places. These were narrower than Seebohm seemed to suggest. Priority was to be given to children

with only one parent;

who need temporary day care on account of the mother's illness;

whose mothers are unable to look after them adequately because they are incapable of giving young children the care they need;

for whom day care might prevent the breakdown of the
mother or the break-up of the family;

whose home conditions constitute a hazard to their
health and welfare;

whose health and welfare are seriously affected by a lack
of opportunity to play with others.

The circular also suggested that local authorities might place
children in private nurseries or with approved child minders,
or in nursery schools, or increase provision by giving help to
voluntary groups. Where these efforts still did not meet the
needs, local authorities could apply to set up part-time
nursery groups, using existing premises and voluntary staff:
child care was still to be done on the cheap.

Local authorities took up these suggestions, and in 1970
the Department of Health and Social Security was able to
state optimistically in its annual report,

During the year there was a marked increase in provision
by local authorities of day care facilities for pre-school
children. By the end of 1970, 439 extra places were
provided in local authority day nurseries and the number
of children with special needs placed by local authorities
in private or voluntary nurseries or playgroups, or with
selected child minders, rose from 658 at the end of 1969
to 1,465 at the end of 1970. In addition, local authorities
were providing 2,373 places in their own part-time nursery
groups, an increase of 790 during the year.

By 1973 the numbers had risen to 829 placements with
child minders, 1,791 in private nurseries, and 3,478 in local
authority part-time nursery groups. This can hardly be regarded
as any real rise in provision as the number of places was barely
increased, children being merely placed through the local
authority instead of privately. However, it is true to say that in
1969 the decline in the number of day nurseries was halted,
and they began to increase (see Figure 4).

By 1973, the picture of day care and education looked
like the table overleaf.

Compared with the same table for 1966 (given earlier)

we can see that there has been a considerable increase in
the numbers and percentage of children in registered forms
of education and care, from 366,297 (9 per cent) to
845,975 (23 per cent) in 1973. Most of this has been due
to the increase in the numbers in primary schools and
in private nursery schools and playgroups, though 3 per
cent of the percentage increase was due to the falling
number of children under five during this period.

Day care and nursery education in 1973 (England and Wales)

	Number of schools, premises or persons	Number of children	% population 0–4 years
Nursery schools	548	42,397	1.1
Under fives in primary schools (nursery and other classes)	not known	351,239	9.4
Day nurseries (run by local authority)	493	25,129	0.7
Private nurseries (inc. playgroups, nurseries, nursery schools)	13,397	335,332	9.0
Registered child minders	30,333	91,878	2.5
TOTAL		845,975	22.7

Local authority part-time groups, direct grant and independent nursery schools are not included. These account
for another 36,698 children. Sources: see Tables 2, 3 and 4.

Trends in development

By 1972, local authority social services had been reorganised
and the Department of Health and Social Security asked for
ten-year development plans from each local authority (circular
35/72). In giving guidance on the provision of day nurseries,
it laid down a target of 8 places per 1,000 children under five
(the current national average level then being 6 places per
1,000). It is not clear why this figure was chosen, as the
circular itself admits that it is probably inadequate.

The ten-year plans to 1983 put in by local authorities

show an immense variation both in their current and estimated expenditure on day nurseries and playgroups (described in Department of Health circular LASSL(74)22). Thus in 1972/3, the Greater London Council area was spending far more than any other region on such services (£9.22 a head of the population under five) whereas the London South Region, for example, was only spending 85p a head. In projected plans, over the five-year period to 1978, the regions which intended to increase their spending the most were Yorkshire (by 229 per cent), London North (203 per cent) and London South (216 per cent), all areas where day nursery provision is now low. The lowest increase in expenditure was proposed by the North-West (76 per cent), which has high day nursery provision, so if these plans go ahead, it may be that some of the regional disparities will decrease. One does not know from these figures, of course, the relative emphasis that will be placed on day nurseries and playgroups.

Unfortunately, in 1974/5 the capital programme for local authority social services departments was cut by 20 per cent overall, and the departmental circular (LASSL(74)22) envisaged that targets put forward in local authorities' ten-year plans would not be reached by 1982. And now, in the present economic climate, it looks as if these plans, limited as they are, will be shelved for some time.

One result of this may be an increase in nurseries and creches provided by places of work. Already pressure is coming from different occupational groups, for example the civil service and universities. The National Union of Students has a campaign for nurseries in all places of higher education. The survey of company day nurseries (Day 1975) found that both employers and trade unions had reservations about expanding their nurseries, particularly over mothers being tied to an employer for a nursery place, but accepted that, in the face of the general lack of provision, expansion was desirable.

Nursery education

Nursery class places have also been affected by the economic situation. Many local authorities have said that they cannot afford to run the additional classes that would be built

89

with the £34 million allocation for the years 1974/76. A report from the National Union of Teachers in 1975 (*Guardian*, 26 March 1975) showed that 24 authorities were not taking up their allocations in full for this reason, and of these 18 were already below the national average in provision for three and four year olds. This means that the rate of expansion planned in Plowden and the White Paper is unlikely to take place: indeed, already in some areas no further development is envisaged for at least the next two years. Most recently, in August 1975, the Department of Education have announced that the building allocation for nursery school building for the year 1976/7 will be £9 million, only half that of the previous years.

5 Provision for the under fives today in England and Wales

The previous chapter looked at the policies and trends in services for the under fives in this century, the growth in particular types of provision and the increasing fragmentation of services. Not that variety and adaptability are undesirable — on the contrary, services should be responsive and appropriate to the differing needs of families. However, the division of responsibility for different forms of provision, the apparent lack of consideration of underlying social trends and the lack of any coherent and comprehensive policy for young children and their families, has given rise to a very uneven and unsatisfactory picture. This chapter will describe in more detail just what the different services are, what they provide, where they are, and who makes use of them. Most of the information is based on official government statistics for 1973 (Department of Health and Social Security 1973, Department of Education and Science, 1975a, 1975b).

Administratively there are two groups of provision, those which are the responsibility of the Department of Health and Social Security, and those which come under the Department of Education and Science. The table shows which services come under each, and the numbers and percentages of children attending in 1973 in England and Wales.

As the table shows, we have information about the way less than a quarter of our children under five spend their day. We know nothing about the remainder, many of whom will be at home with their mothers, some cared for by relatives or friends, and others by unregistered child minders or other paid help. There are some things we know about the 23 per cent of children attending registered or public services, though by no means as much as we should. Before we discuss this, a brief description is given of the various forms of provision and the

Department of Health and Social Security

	Number of children	% (0—4)
493 local authority day nurseries	25,129	0.7
109 local authority part-time nursery groups	3,968	0.1
13,323 private and voluntary nurseries, nursery schools, playgroups	333,076	8.9
74 factory nurseries and crèches	2,256	0.1
30,333 child-minders (possibly including some playgroups)	91,878	2.5
TOTAL	456,307	12.2

Department of Education and Science

	Number of children	% (0—4)
548 nursery schools (maintained)	42,397*	1.1
124 nursery schools (direct grant and independent)	5,662	0.2
2,149 nursery classes in maintained primary schools	81,559	2.2
Other classes in maintained primary schools	269,680	7.2
Other independent schools	27,068	0.7
TOTAL	426,366	11.4

GRAND TOTAL 882,673

(23.6 per cent of total population 0—4, which was 3,733,100)

*This number includes all children in nursery schools, a few of whom are over five.
Sources: Department of Education and Science, 1975a; Department of Health and Social Security, 1973.

different types of service they offer. This can be very important as it largely determines who can make use of them.

SERVICES PROVIDED BY LOCAL AUTHORITIES

Social Services Departments

Guidance on standards for the day care of young children — covering numbers of children admitted and staff required; the general care, health and feeding of children; and the training needs of staff — is provided in Ministry of Health circular 37/68, which covers local authority as well as private and voluntary day-care provision.

Day nurseries are run for children aged up to four years (though some do not provide for babies) whose mothers are unable to look after them during the day or who would benefit on health or certain social grounds. The categories of children eligible for admission are given in Ministry of Health circular 37/68, which says that 'priority will normally need to be given to children with only one parent who has no option but to go out to work'. Day nurseries are open for long hours each day (usually 8.30 am to 5.30 or 6 pm) and most, though not all, children attend full-time. They are open all year round and are staffed by nursery nurses and assistants under the direction of a matron, and do not normally have qualified teachers on the staff. A staff:child ratio of 1:5 is recommended, more if there is a high proportion of children under two. A charge is made to parents according to means.

Part-time nursery groups are similar in operation to playgroups, being open for short hours during the day and closing for holidays. Circular 37/68 lays down that these may be provided where 'the extent of private or voluntary provision may be insufficient to meet the needs of priority children' and the circular makes it clear that local authorities should use their powers to assist voluntary organisations in preference to setting up their own playgroup provision. An adult:child ratio of 1:8 is recommended where the children are over two. In 1973, one-third of the 108 part-time nursery groups provided by local authorities were in the Greater London area. Some local authorities do not charge, others ask only for a token contribution.

93

Nursery schools are separate, specially equipped schools for the education of children aged two to four years, though most pupils are aged three or four. They operate a normal school day, from about 9.30 am to about 3.30 pm, and are closed during school holidays. About two-thirds of the children attend part-time, that is for a morning or afternoon session, the rest staying for the whole school day, usually including lunch. They are under the direction of a head teacher, and the qualified teaching staff are usually assisted by trained nursery nurses and assistants and unqualified staff. Nationally the ratio of qualified teaching staff to pupils is 1:23 but this is increased to 1:10 when nursery assistants and other adults are taken into account. No charge is made to parents, except for lunch.

Nursery classes are specially equipped and staffed classes for children under five in schools which are not nursery schools, that is, in primary or infant schools. Children under three are rarely admitted and over 60 per cent are part-time. A nursery class teacher should be assisted by at least one full-time nursery assistant or two NNEB students (nursery nurses). Information about exact ratios of teachers or adults to children is not available, but it is a disturbing fact that, with the current emphasis on part-time nursery schooling, one teacher can have charge of up to 30 children in the morning and a different 30 in the afternoon — a total of 60 individual children and their families to try to know.

The position can be even worse in *other classes in primary schools*. These are normally reception or first-year classes in primary schools and are where the majority of under-fives in school are to be found (270,000 pupils in 1973). About half the intake in these classes is of rising fives, that is four year olds who are admitted a term before that in which they will be five; they will therefore be aged four and a half or more. No official information or statistics are available about numbers, staffing or type of educational experience in these classes, but the teachers do not necessarily have appropriate nursery teacher training; they are unlikely to have the help of nursery assistants (in 1973 there were only 3,171 nursery assistants in these classes); the classrooms may be poorly equipped for children of this age, both in terms of work material and room for play and rest; and there may be a double shift system with its resulting disadvantages, as described already. Because it is a cheap form of provision it is becoming increasingly available as the numbers of over-fives in primary schools decrease; and it gives rise to deep concern about the development of our nursery education programme.

SERVICES RUN PRIVATELY OR BY VOLUNTARY BODIES

Nurseries, playgroups and child minders are covered by the Nurseries and Child Minders Regulation Act 1948 as amended by Section 60 of the Health Services and Public Health Act (1968). The guidance on standards for the day care of young children in Ministry of Health circular 37/68 applies also to these provisions, which have to be registered with the local authority Social Services Department. This Department is also expected to visit from time to time, though the offical guidance here (circular 36/68) is that the frequency of such visits should be according to circumstances (that is, at local authority discretion). Ministry of Health circular 36/68 gives guidance to local authorities on such matters as registration and supervision.

Private nurseries include *nursery 'schools'* not registered as educational establishments by the Department of Education and Science; private or voluntary *day nurseries*; and most *playgroups*. The staffing, management, hours of opening and costs to parents therefore vary widely.

Playgroups can vary in the numbers they take from 6 to 40 children (according to Parry and Archer, 1974). They meet regularly for half-day (2½ hour) sessions as a rule, though many are open only two to three times a week and not all children come every time. They are run either by a parents' committee, or by an *ad hoc* group of mothers themselves, and either for profit or, more commonly, on a cooperative basis with or without a grant from the public funds. Most charge parents for each session the child attends, and wherever possible parents are encouraged to help looking after the children, taking turns to do so. In some groups this is essential. The larger playgroups have trained staff in addition.

Private day nurseries offer long hours, including all-day care. They will often take children under two; are often run for profit; rely almost wholly on paid staff to run the provision; and can be expensive.

Local authorities may place and pay for 'priority group' children in such private or voluntary provision and in 1973, in England, there were 1,745 children so placed in day nurseries and 3,448 in part-time provision. A few local authorities rely entirely on placing children in privately run nurseries or groups and have no day care facilities of their own.

A small number of registered private nurseries are attached to factories or work places, for the children of employees. In 1973, 70 out of 74 of these factory nurseries provided all-day care. The lowest age children are taken in them varies, as does the cost of a place, though the nurseries are often subsidised by the companies.

Child minders. Anyone looking after someone else's child under five in their own home must register with the local Social Services Department if payment is made, if the child is not a close relative, and if it is looked after during the day' for at least two hours and for at least one day a week. As with private nurseries, minders have to reach certain minimum standards in safety and facilities for the local authority to register them. Ministry of Health circular 37/68 also recommends that a single-handed minder should not normally have more than three children under five, including any of her own; and in registering a minder, the local authority usually lays down a maximum number of children to be taken.

Children are usually taken all day and the cost varies, but is normally several pounds a week. Local authorities can place and pay for 'priority group' children, and in 1973, in England, 826 children were being minded in this way.

It is acknowledged that many child minders are not registered, so there is no really accurate estimate of the numbers of children cared for in other people's homes. The official statistics, covering legal, registered provision only, are also confusing, since some playgroups are registered under this 'minder' category and they account for a large proportion of the 4,710 'registered persons providing sessional care only' in England in 1973.

A small amount of privately organised nursery provision is regarded as educational in aim and is therefore registered under the Education Acts. This comprises:

Direct grant and independent nursery schools. Nursery schools that want to be registered as educational establishments have to be registered under section 70 of the 1944 Education Act. This involves the schools meeting certain minimum requirements in such matters as premises, instruction and staff. These minimum requirements are not in fact laid down and a decision on each application is made to the Department of Education following the report of a visit made by a Department Inspector. Independent schools can further seek recognition as efficient, which requires meeting certain higher standards, a decision again being made by the Department on the basis of their Inspector's report. There are three types of non-maintained nursery schools: (a) *direct grant,* providing for 567 children at the end of 1972, nearly 60 per cent of whom were full time; (b) *independent schools recognised as efficient*, providing for 527 children at the end of 1972, less than 30 per cent of whom were full-time; (c) *independent schools, registered but not recognised*, providing for 4,568 children at the end of 1972, just over half of whom were full-time. Apart from direct grant schools, some of whose pupils have free places, all those schools charge parents, though the amount will vary.

CHARACTERISTICS OF CHILDREN PROVIDED FOR

Having described the forms of care and education available, this chapter now returns to a more detailed account of the children and families who use these different services, how some of the services have developed, and where they are to be found.

Age of children
Of all the forms of day care, only local authority day

nurseries, some private nurseries, factory nurseries and child minders will consider caring for very young children, since in 1973 resources were withheld by the Department of Education for the expansion of nursery education for children under three years. Day nurseries therefore have a special task to care for children up to two years, there being no other statutory provision for them; but in fact no information is available about the ages of children in day nurseries, or in private nurseries or with child minders. Playgroups do sometimes admit children from the age of two, but again, no information is available nationally about the age of children who actually attend. A recent survey of 26 company/factory nurseries (Day, 1975) showed that 12 out of 22 did not take children before the age of two. We therefore simply do not know how many children in this youngest age group are being cared for outside the home, or how they are being looked after.

In nursery education, the scene is very well documented, and returns by age are filed each year by local education authorities. In primary schools, four year olds have since the second world war been the largest age group under five, and two and three year olds have always been very low in numbers. In 1973, of the under-fives in classes in primary schools, under ½ per cent were aged two, 9½ per cent were three, 41½ per cent were four and 49 per cent were rising five (children who became five in the spring term in which the statistics were collected). Most expansion seems to have taken place in the numbers of rising-fives admitted to school, possibly as the numbers in primary schools began to fall and space became available. Rising-fives are nearly all in classes other than nursery classes, that is in reception classes or in the first year class. Figure 5 shows the changing age pattern amongst under-fives in primary schools since 1947. The proportion of two year olds is too small to show: in 1947 there were only 953 two year old pupils, and in 1973 only 739.

Numbers in separate maintained nursery schools are very small compared with those under-fives in primary schools (42,000 against 351,000) but the age structure is very different. There are very few rising-fives (only 1,342 in

98

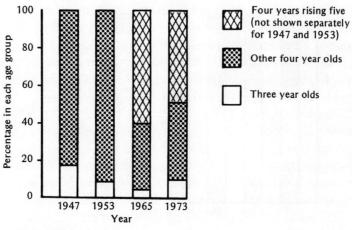

Figure 5: Age distribution of pupils under five in maintained primary schools (England & Wales)

See Table 5

1973) and the rest are split almost evenly between three and other four year olds with 5 per cent aged two. Figure 6 shows the change since 1947, the most noticeable trend being the decline in the proportion of two year olds. In comparison with the state sector (393,000 children) the number of under fives in private, independent schools is very small — 32,730 in 1973, of whom only 5,662 were in separate nursery schools.

Figure 6: Age distribution of children in maintained nursery schools (England & Wales)

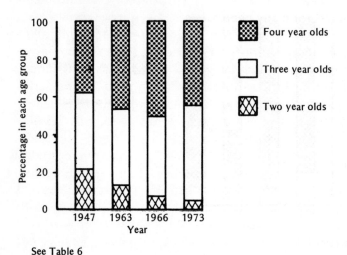

See Table 6

In total, in 1973, in state nursery schools, classes in primary schools, special schools, and private schools, the proportion of each age group at school was as follows (taken from figures of the Department of Education and Science, 1975):

Age	% of age group in school	
2	0.6	Total: 18.6% of
3	8.3	age group 2—4
4	46.2	

Full and part-time provision

This is a crucial aspect of provision, affecting the sort of children and families who are able to take up the different services. A service which is only available a few hours each day, or which closes for long holidays, is of little use to a working mother, even in part-time work, or for those who have to travel a considerable distance, or for mothers or children who need sustained and regular support. However, the fastest growing form of provision over the last few years has been playgroups. Nearly all of these are open only for a few hours a day, most close for holidays and many expect some level of parental involvement, all of which limit their usefulness for many people.

There are four types of provision offering full-time, all-year day care: local authority day nurseries, some factory day nurseries, some private day nurseries and most child minders. In 1973 in England and Wales, local authority day nurseries had 23,838 places, and private and factory nurseries had 25,247 full-time places, enough to provide for only 1.3 per cent of the under-fives. Local authority nurseries are restricted to definite categories of families and children regarded as being in special need (see Chapter 4). Factory nurseries are few and almost entirely limited to employees; and private nurseries are limited in number and, for many people, costly. Considering that registered child minders who look after children *all day* (those who provide 'sessional' care have not been counted here) provide for only another 1.5 per cent of under-fives (57,042 children), there is only known to be full-time day care provision for 106,127 children (2.8 per cent of under-fives). There is therefore an enormous short-fall between what is available and the most conservative estimates of need — and certainly desire — for this sort of provision.

Although accurate data about this demand are abysmally lacking, some indication of the pressure on this limited day-time provision can be seen by looking at the few figures available from local authority, census and other returns.

Number of children regarded as priority cases
on the waiting lists of local authority day
nurseries (England and Wales, 1973)   9,899

Number of children under five in one-
parent families (Great Britain, 1971)   260,000

Number of women with children under
five working 30 or more hours a week
(Great Britain 1971)   175,700

(Taken respectively from Department of Health and Social
Security, 1973; Committee on One-Parent Families, 1974;
Census, 1971.)

Of course, some of these categories overlap, but even if the
number of day nursery places is increased to the target of 8
places per 1,000 children under five, this would only result
in approximately 30,000 places, by no means enough for
those children we know about. In addition, there are other
children in the categories laid down, for whom day nursery
places should be available — children in overcrowded
housing, in flats in high blocks, without play space, those
whose mothers are physically or mentally unable to cope,
or whose families have disintegrated, children with minor
handicaps or developmental problems, or whose health
and welfare is threatedned through lack of opportunities
for play and contact with other children. We do not even
have the roughest estimate of how many are involved.

Full time nursery schooling is not all-day care, as in
day nurseries. There are usually two sessions, one in the
morning and one in the afternoon, of about two and a
half hours each, though most children stay for lunch
in between. There are also the long school holidays. It
cannot be regarded, therefore, as full-time provision,
and unless combined with some other form of care — from
a relative, friend, paid minder, etc. — it is not suited to the
needs of mothers with a regular job outside the home.

Part-time education, for a morning or afternoon session
of about two and a half hours is barely enough time to go
to the launderette. However this is now the way nursery
education is to develop. It is the stated government
view that two or so hours away from mother is as much as
most children can take, and this is all most of them are
going to get. Although the circular setting out this policy

102

Figure 7: Pupils and places in primary and nursery schools (England & Wales)

Under-five pupils and places in primary schools

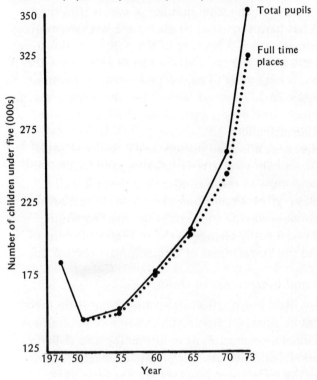

Pupils and places in nursery schools

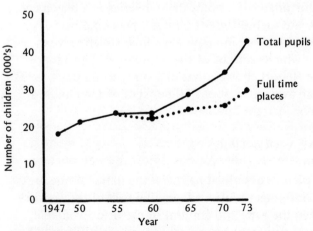

See Tables 3 and 4

did not come till 1973, the trend towards part-time schooling was already very clear in nursery schools. In them the growth of part-time pupils at the expense of full-time schooling is particularly marked: the total number of *places* (full-time equivalent) has hardly risen at all during the last twenty-five years. In primary schools because of the policy of admitting rising-fives full time, the change is not so dramatic, but the same pattern is beginning to emerge, especially in separate nursery classes. In 1973, there were 2,149 nursery classes in primary schools, and 84 per cent of the children in them were part-time attenders.

Nationally, in maintained nursery and primary schools, 76 per cent of under-fives attend full time, and 24 per cent part time, and most of these children are rising five. But though with very few exceptions, all education authorities have more under-fives at school full-time than part-time, this should presumably change as the recommendations of Plowden and the Department of Education are carried out.

Social class and background of children

There is very little information about this. What little there is shows that in nursery schools, the children of professional and non-manual workers are over-represented and skilled manual workers' children are marginally less likely to be attending — the differences however are not very great. (Central Statistical Office, 1974). The other available figures unfortunately combine day nurseries and playgroups, and as they are such different services, the combined figures are of little use in helping to show which services are used by which sections of the population. The Finer Committee Report showed that in a study of 68 day nurseries, an average of about 50 per cent of the children were from one-parent families.

REGIONAL VARIATIONS

So far the picture described has been the national one, but there are enormous variations from one part of the country to another in the type and amount of provision available, usually for no apparent reason other than the different

104

emphasis placed on day care and education of children by different local authorities.

Day care

The haphazard arrangement of local authority day nurseries is probably due in part to the differences in the speed with which they were closed down or transferred to education after the war. It would be logical to expect more provision in the more densely populated and industrialised areas, firstly because social stress giving rise to the conditions under which children are admitted to day nurseries (for example, bad housing) is more likely to arise here, and secondly, because where the population is scattered or small, it is less feasible to set up day nurseries because there are just not enough children within easy travelling distance to make it worthwhile.

On the whole, this is what we find. Under the old county boundaries in 1973, administrative counties had less provision than county boroughs. All, except Cheshire and Lancashire, were below the national average of 6 places per 1,000 children, and 33 out of 58 counties had no local authority day nursery provision at all. By contrast, of the 116 London and county boroughs, only 16 were below average and only 24 had no provision at all. Wales was particularly badly provided for, only Cardiff and Newport in the south having any nurseries. Almost as badly off was Southern and South East England with a total of only 17 day nurseries, 2 places per 1,000 children: Central England (Bedfordshire, Berkshire, Buckinghamshire, Cambridgeshire, Hertfordshire, Huntingdonshire, Oxfordshire and East Anglia) also only had 2 places per 1,000 followed by the South West with 3 places per 1,000. The authorities with the most provision were Inner London, which had 28 places per 1,000 children, and the North West with 12 per 1,000.

There is nothing to show whether these variations correspond to different needs in different parts of the country, though it is certainly true that rural areas have a lower rate of working mothers while London and the North West are both high, and also have housing and other social problems.

It is important also when thinking about future

developments, to look at population movements. The declining birth-rate and migration are causing the population of large cities to fall; and the group that is moving out is the 30—39 age group, those likely to have young families. The areas which are receiving this population are not so much the suburbs of large towns and conurbations, as smaller towns, new towns and rural districts. Thus East Anglia, the South West and part of the South East increased their share of the population of England and Wales from 18.8 per cent to 20.4 per cent in the ten years from 1961 to 1971 (Eversley, 1974). It is precisely these areas which are particularly badly provided for in local authority day care.

Of the total of 74 factory nurseries, 23 are in the North West and in West Yorkshire, these being the areas with long traditions of female labour. The South West and Wales only have one between them. In the survey of company day nurseries (Day, 1975) the most frequently mentioned reasons for setting up the nursery were shortage of staff, the wish of women employees with children to continue working and lack of suitable local authority facilities.

The amount of full-time provision in private day nurseries is almost exactly the same as that in local authority day nurseries (6 places per 1,000 children). However, the distribution is rather different. Although the large cities are again relatively well provided, the industrial North West has very few private nurseries and the South, South East, Central and Eastern counties are well above the average — exactly the reverse picture to that for local authority nurseries. It is probable that the private market stepped in to fill the gap.

Playgroups and part-time nurseries

These fall within the responsibility of Social Services Departments and are classified as part of the day care provisions. However, as has already been described, they are normally open only for short periods and not always every day. The national average in 1973 was 83 places per 1,000 population under five; and overall, county areas tend to be better provided for than towns and county boroughs. The big cities, which have a high level of full-time day nursery provision, are well below average in playgroups as are the industrial North West and the North East with 54 places per 1,000. Wales, too, is short of such groups throughout the country. Conversely, the areas of highest provision are those where day nursery places are few — the South West (110 places per 1,000), South and South East (123 places), Central England and most of East Anglia.

There could be several reasons for these variations: (1) In areas of high levels of female employment, or social stress, the few hours provided by a playgroup are not appropriate to local needs, but county areas have fewer working mothers. (2) Playgroups are organised on a semi-formal, very local basis and do not need special buildings or staff. They can therefore adapt more easily to the facilities available in county areas. (3) If one looks at the expansion of playgroups as a reaction to the paucity of places in nursery schools, then there should be more playgroups where there are few nursery places. This seems to be true: nearly all the areas with high levels of playgroup provision (for example, the South, South West, South East and Central England) are below average in their level of nursery schooling; whereas the places with fewer playgroups (for example, the cities, the North East and the North West), have more schooling, particularly full time places, for the under-fives.

Education

Nationally there are 83 full-time places per 1,000 children, and 23 part-time places, for children between two and four years of age in all maintained schools. Welsh local education authorities, with the exception of Swansea, have most of all, ranging from 98 to 294 places per 1,000, mostly full-time. There was no education authority in 1973 which did not have any provision in schools for under-fives . Out of the 172 education authorities, only 13 had no separate nursery schools or classes but accommodated their under-fives in other classes in primary schools. These did not admit three year olds.

Earlier on in the chapter we looked at the age distribution in nursery schools and classes and found a preponderance of four year olds and rising-fives in primary school classes (over 90 per cent) but a more even split between three and four year olds in separate nursery schools, with very few two year olds anywhere. Forty-seven local education authorities have all three types — nursery schools, nursery classes, and other classes in primary schools. Some local education authorities, particularly in Central and Southern England, and South Wales, concentrate on admitting the rising-fives; in some cases over 90 per cent of the under-fives in school are of this age. On the other hand, the Welsh counties and many towns in the North West and North East, admit comparatively low proportions of rising-fives, which means more places for the three year olds.

Apart from these very broad distinctions, the balance of age groups in pre-schooling seems to be very much a question of local policy. The more separate nursery schools there are, the more three year olds are likely to get a place, though there are authorities which admit large numbers of three year olds to their nursery classes in primary schools. Nowhere is there more than a handful of two year olds in primary school classes, and even in separate nursery schools only 5 per cent of the children are aged two (most of them are likely to be nearer three than two years). Only about 20 education authorities in England and Wales admit a higher proportion than this, from 6 per cent to 46 per cent in one case, nearly all in Wales and the Northern half of England. The actual numbers involved are often very small. This age group distribution corresponds fairly closely to the total number of places available for under-fives; where there are few places, preference is given to admitting older children, and only where nursery school provision is considerably higher than the national average do three year olds get much chance of a place.

COSTS AND STAFFING

Comparisons in cost between day nurseries and nursery education are difficult to make because they are run and financed in different ways, and it is not possible to get at any figure for the under-five component in primary schools. Costs for nursery schooling also include fees paid by authorities for children in private and direct grant schools.

108

It is however useful to give some overall indication of the level of spending, and comparisons as far as possible, bearing in mind the dangers of doing this. Also to be borne in mind are the hidden costs and benefits of pre-school provision. For example, many mothers can go out to work during the day if their children are looked after; they then become tax payers, contribute to national insurance funds and produce goods or services; families with low incomes might be claiming social security benefits if the wife did not work; mothers who just cannot cope with children all day may be saved from mental or physical breakdown and the resultant necessity to take children into care. With this in mind, the table shows some total costs for the two services in England and Wales.

Total net local authority expenditure 1972/3	Day nurseries	Nursery schools
Current costs, inc. loan charges and less fees from parents (day nurseries only)	£9,490,167	£7,637,000
Staff costs as % of the total	77%	78%
Cost per full-time place	£398	£262

Sources: Department of Education and Science 1975b; Department of Health and Social Security 1973; Department of Health and Social Security unpublished figures.

The adult:child ratio in day nurseries in 1973 was 1:4, and in maintained nursery schools was 1:10. The teacher:child ratio in nursery schools was 1:22 (Department of Education and Science, 1975b). The higher cost of day nurseries is largely due to the number of staff needed to keep nurseries open long daily hours and throughout the year (though salaries are much lower than for nursery school staff), and the higher staff:child ratio necessary for care of children under two. A certain amount of day care costs are recovered from parents who are required to pay according to their means; this covers 8 per cent of the running costs in Inner London, 17 per cent in county boroughs and 20 per cent in county council areas. (The cost of administering this means-test system is not known.) In money terms this amounts to an average of 21 pence a day to 37 pence in the counties (Chartered Institute of Public Finance and Accountancy, 1974; all other information about day nursery costs also comes from this source). The average daily amounts paid in individual local authority areas varies even more, from 9 pence a day in Oxfordshire to 77 pence a day in Sunderland.

Most of the cost of a day nursery place is incurred in paying the staff, but here again there is a wide national variation, and staff costs can be 70 per cent higher in one authority than another, even discounting London. Presumably this is due to child:staff ratios which do differ from place to place, to the level of qualifications held by staff which affects their pay, and to the number of very young children under two who require a higher staff ratio.

Capital costs of new day nurseries are normally borrowed, from central government or elsewhere, so part of the yearly cost of running a day nursery is the interest which has to be paid on the loan. Nationally this amounts to between 6 and 7½ per cent of the total cost per child-day. However, very few nurseries have been built since the war, and central government money has only been available for expansion since 1972. For this reason, many local authorities have no capital charges to pay at all, having expanded their services little since the war. This applies particularly to the industrial towns of Lancashire and Cheshire and to some other counties which took advantage of Treasury money available during the war for building day nurseries. Where new nurseries are built, capital charges will represent a considerable proportion of yearly costs, and must deter many local authorities, who are under increasing financial pressure, from expanding this type of provision, regardless of how much money is available on loan. For example, the average national running costs per child-day are £2.04, excluding capital charges, yet in 1973, one local authority was paying as much as £2 a child-day in capital charges, in addition to running costs.

It is clearly important, costs being as high as they are, that maximum use is made of the facilities provided. However the occupancy rate of day nurseries does drop very low — to

110

60 per cent in one case. There clearly has to be a little slack in the system to allow for emergency admissions, illness, temporary absence, but this should be as little as possible, and an under use of 20 to 25 per cent or more, which is quite common, is surely too high. If this is the usual absence rate, then it should be possible to add more children to the register to achieve an actual occupancy rate nearer 100 per cent.

CONCLUSIONS

Registered private and public provision looks after 24 per cent of the nation's under-fives during some part of their day when they are not with their mothers. For these few it varies from child minder to local authority day nursery, from playgroup to nursery class, and less than half this provision is made by the public sector.

Nationally we know almost nothing about what happens to the remaining children — nearly 3 million of them — about their lives and the lives of their parents. Many will be at home with mother, others cared for by relatives and friends and other private arrangements. How is the 24 per cent we do know about selected, or self-selected? A lot will depend on luck and local policy; some will be able to buy what they need. For the very young child, up to three years of age, there is very little provision indeed, and the government has no plans to increase the care for this group to any appreciable extent, despite the fact that they are the ones who cause most concern. Over three the prospect is brighter — nursery schooling on demand, and free, has been accepted as a principle, though development, in the current economic climate, is in jeopardy. Because of its part-time nature it is also of little use to many thousands of parents, and some nursery classes cannot fill their part-time places because they do not meet the local need.

Care and education for young children is expensive — but so is the education of secondary school pupils and undergraduates, and even more so the care of young people and families who fall by the wayside. Succeeding chapters will discuss some of the results of *not* providing adequate child care and education services, and the increasing awareness of the need to do so.

111

The 1972 White Paper on education (Department of
Education and Science, 1972) pointed out how low the level
of provision for under-fives was in this country compared
with that in other European countries. It might therefore
be instructive to see how we do compare with them in the
amount and type of provision we make, and possibly in
what directions our future development might lie. We have
studied a selection of Western European countries — Belgium,
France, Germany, Italy, the Netherlands, Denmark, Norway
and Sweden — for which recent information was available in
reliable translation.

Before going on to the actual descriptions, several points
need making. First, the age of compulsory schooling is in all
cases higher than it is in this country; in the Netherlands,
Denmark and Sweden it is seven, and in the others six. This
obviously means that there are far more older children to be
catered for in pre-school services. Secondly, the clear
distinction between private and state or local authority
provision is not made as it is here. This is particularly true in
those countries like France, Belgium, Italy and the
Netherlands, where the church has always been prominent in
education. In these cases, unless the service is run for a profit
(which is rare) it is regarded as part of the national provision,
subject to a degree of state supervision and usually subsidised
in the same way as state-run provision, so that in practice
there is little difference between private and state provision.
Indeed, in Italy, which has much nursery schooling, there was
no state pre-school system before 1968. In some countries,
such as Belgium and the Netherlands, the different churches
and interests compete with each other and against the falling
birth-rate to enrol children in nursery services — which have

burgeoned in consequence. Thirdly, the sources for the information in this chapter vary in detail and explanation, so in some cases it is difficult to give a complete picture and to make direct comparisons with the types of provision in this country (OECD, 1972, 1973, 1974; Rosengren, 1973; Commission of the European Communities, 1975; official statistics supplied by embassies).

Belgium

Compulsory school entry age is six. Nursery schools take children from two or three to five and are open for a fairly long day (8.30 am to 4.15 pm or later) to look after the children of working mothers. They are free, whether state or privately run. Over 90 per cent of three to five year olds attend, and in 1973, 23 per cent of two year olds were in school. School, as well as benefiting the child, is seen as a means of social equalisation. Nursery schools have expanded since the war and especially since 1958 when the state began to build or subsidise 'neutral' (culturally and religiously unbiased) schools. The government view is that under the age of three education as such is not necessary, though this is being criticised. Provision is made for children from nought to two of single or working mothers, in creches (roughly equivalent to our day nurseries), with *gardiennes* (child minders, some of whom are attached to and paid through creches) and private day nurseries. Altogether there were 27,427 places of such types (12,000 of these were with child minders). This is a fairly low level of provision but it is estimated that it catered for 37 per cent of working women with children. Government concern has been expressed at the low level of provision for this age group and it is envisaged that future expansion will be in the subsidised child minders attached to creches.

France

Public and private education for three to five year olds is free, and schools are open for long hours (8 am to 6.30 pm) though the formal education component only lasts six hours, and the service of care provided at the beginning and end of the day is paid for by those who want it. A very high proportion of children attend school, 23 per cent of two year olds, 70 per cent of three year olds, 93 per cent at four and 96 per cent at five. Pre-school education has always been regarded seriously and has been steadily expanding.

A great number of mothers in France have always worked. Different systems of child care before nursery school age have developed, and a complex system of subsidies and allowances exists to enable women to obtain care for their children. For example, in 1972 a Child Minding Allowance was introduced for all families with children under three, according to specific criteria. Most of the need is met by community creches, for children under three years, some privately run, some municipally, but all approved and subsidised. Places in such creches increased by 66 per cent between 1965 and 1972 to reach a level of 32,828 places (13 per 1,000 infants). There was a target of 150,000 places by 1975.

It is estimated that two-thirds of places in community creches are taken by children from middle-class one-child families where the mother has a stable job, and that working-class mothers use the other main form of provision, family creches. This is a system of individuals who take children into their homes, like our child minders. They are often chosen by the municipality, are under the supervision of a matron of a community creche, and are paid by the agency that manages that creche. Numbers here doubled in the year 1972/3. Another form of pre-school provision (now decreasing in number) consists of child care centres and kindergartens for children aged three to five; they look after children during the day, and lay emphasis on care and physical development.

The lack of continuity of care between creche and school, and the absence of coherent policy and clear goals has recently led to an experiment in setting up 'Early Childhood Centres' to offer a full range of flexible services.

Germany (Federal Republic)
School is compulsory in Germany at the age of six and it is only over the last decade or so that there has been much expansion in services for pre-school children. There are currently about 5.5 million children under six, of whom 2.5

million are under three. At a Federal level, the Ministry of Youth, Family and Health, and in particular the Youth Welfare Service, is responsible for pre-school services, though most of the responsibility for policy, law and funding lies with the eleven *Lände* (states). Also involved at state and local level are the Voluntary Unions of Youth Welfare Services. 75 per cent of kindergartens (nursery schools) are operated by voluntary agencies, subject to state inspection. There is little practical distinction between voluntary and state operated services which are both counted as part of the national provision and subsidised by the state and local government. Pre-school provision is almost entirely restricted to nursery schools for children aged three to five. Parents pay according to their income and a maximum fee is set by law. Nursery schools are normally only open for half a day, as are elementary schools. Full day care is provided in some nursery schools, and for the under-threes in day nurseries, which again parents pay for according to their means.

In 1973 about 44 per cent of children aged three to five were attending nursery school, compared to 34 per cent in 1968. The number of places in nursery schools almost doubled between 1960 and 1973 (from 805,000 to 1,440,000). In 1972 the nursery school population consisted of 17 per cent of all three year olds, 39 per cent of four year olds, 54 per cent of five year olds and 53 per cent of six year olds (prior to entering primary schools).

Numbers in day nurseries are very much smaller. In 1973 there were 653 nurseries with 20,428 places, catering for less than one per cent of the under-three population. As there are neither enough day nursery or nursery school places to go round, children are selected according to certain priorities, and in accordance with their age and place on the waiting list. Priority is given to the children of working mothers and one-parent families, deprived children and where parents are for other reasons unable to look after their children.

Although there are only 20,000 nursery places for under-threes, and 140,000 full day places in nursery schools for three to five year olds, there are about 800,000 children under six with working mothers. However, the extended family system is still important in Germany and some 40 per cent of children of working mothers have grandparents living in the same household. It is hoped that by 1980 there will be nursery school places for all three to five year olds who want them, which in 1972 was estimated to be 75 per cent of the age group. Emphasis is therefore on expanding this provision and little is planned for the younger age group, though there is some discussion and experimentation in family day care. There are also suggestions that the Ministry of Culture and the Ministry of Social Affairs should be jointly responsible for pre-school facilities and programmes.

The Netherlands

The compulsory school entry age is seven, although many are admitted while still six. Nursery schooling is restricted to four to six year olds, but nearly all of this age group attend — in 1973, 88 per cent of four year olds, 96 per cent of five year olds and almost all six year olds were receiving schooling. Nursery schools are open for three hours in the morning and two hours in the afternoon, and not all children go each day. Even in 1900, there were 1,000 schools taking children under compulsory school age, and in 1972 there were 6,600 such schools. The religious denominations have always provided much of the education, and in 1973 ran about 60 per cent of the nursery schools. All are subsidised, and there is a struggle to enrol as many children as possible. Publicly run schools charge a nominal fee, and privately run schools charge a slightly higher but still fairly low fee. There is very little provision for children before the age of four. Day care centres were started in 1870 for the children of unmarried mothers, and since the 1950s there has been more demand from working and student mothers. Provision is still at a very low level and mostly only in cities, but the number of working mothers in the Netherlands is relatively low too. However, in 1967 the playgroup movement began to take hold, and middle-class mothers began to set up part-time groups for their two and three year olds. In 1970, the day care centres and playgroups joined forces under an organisation known as WKN which in 1973 had 1,000 'kindercentra', 70 taking children all day, and the rest

116

part-time. Fees vary and depend on how often the child attends.

There are two current issues in Dutch pre-school provision: one is how to integrate nursery and primary schools, which are physically and in teaching aim quite far apart, and the other is whether to lower the age of entrance to nursery school to three.

Italy

Before 1968, the government had no resources to put into pre-school provision, and most of this was provided by religious organisations. The availability of nursery schooling was none the less good, nearly 50 per cent of children aged three to five being able to attend. Since public nursery schools were started in 1968, another 10 per cent of children now attend, and the target is 86 per cent by 1978. Fees vary, public schools are free, but hours are often shorter and more inflexible than in private schools. Private schools are state subsidised and either charge for meals and transport only, or for enrolment as well. They are usually open for long hours, often till 6 pm. Day care before the age of three is much more variable and depends very much on local demand. Again, until 1971, it was almost entirely private. In that year a law was passed and a five-year plan drawn up to build 3,800 creches sufficient for 7 per cent of that age group; it is however unlikely that this target will be reached through lack of money. Recently, private provision, which had begun to decline, has started to expand in the face of state competition. In 1972 there were some 560 state creches and 200 private creches catering for about 1 per cent of the under-three population.

Denmark

In Denmark, compulsory school entry age is seven, although about 65 per cent of six year olds are in pre-school. This has been achieved mainly through the expansion since 1966 in kindergarten classes in primary schools which admit six year olds for 15 hours a week; 40 per cent of six year olds are in such classes, and another 25 per cent are in separate nursery schools. Nursery schools admit children from the age of two, although there are few in this age group. About 27 per cent of three to six year olds are in nursery school, all are subsidised, but two-thirds are privately run. Payment is made according to earnings and about a quarter of the places are free. For younger children, day care is provided in subsidised day nurseries; about 7 per cent of children up to two are looked after here (15,700 children) and another 21,000 children are in wholly private creches or with day foster mothers. Social factors are not considered in allocating pre-school places, but it is envisaged that the public sector will expand in small towns and rural areas where the level of provision is now low.

Norway

Norway on the other hand, is planning to increase its pre-school provision for social and economic reasons. Priority is given to working mothers, single-parent families and children with 'low level cultural background'. It is envisaged that more mothers will go out to work as the needs of the labour market expand, as families get smaller and as education improves. The level of pre-school provision in 1972 was very low, a total of 5 per cent of children under school age attending some form of provision. Nursery schools are for three to six year olds and are part time; some six year olds attend pre-school classes which are 'school readiness' classes in primary schools. Other day care is divided into centres for the under-threes and the over-threes. In 1972 there were only 1,839 places in day care centres for under-threes.

Sweden

Sweden is working towards an integrated system of child centres where care and education are combined under the same ministerial responsibility.

Day nurseries developed very slowly until the mid-sixties and private family nurseries provided the most care. The main impetus to public expansion has been the changing attitudes to collective child rearing and to women's role, plus an increasing number of mothers going out to work. Nursery and play schools increased rapidly during the fifties, doubling their intake in that decade. By the 1960s, the labour market was expanding and there was increasing pressure for day care facilities. Several commissions and study groups were set up during the 1960s to look at various aspects of provision, and in 1968 a Commission on Child Centres was set up with a very wide remit to consider the form and content of pre-school facilities, and how they should expand. It affirmed the importance of pre-school as part of community life and a complement to the family, and stressed that the only difference between the forms of facilities should be the number of hours available and ages accepted, not the content and purpose. Day nurseries and nursery schools were all to be regarded as pre-school centres; all staff should have educational duties. Expansion was first to be based on the right of all children to attend pre-school a year or more before compulsory schooling (which does not start until the age of seven). Children with handicaps were made a priority group and were to have the right to pre-schooling from the age of four. The aim is that pre-school shall meet the demands of parents, and in the long term be offered to children from an early age; in the meantime, working or student parents should have the first claim on places. A timetable was set out to meet these targets, and local authorities invited to put in their plans. A common administration of pre-schooling was proposed since it was thought very important that the services should not be split between Social Services and Education; experimental joint bodies were set up at local level.

Until the fully coordinated system is developed, there are still many different kinds of provision for pre-school children. Nursery schools and play schools are provided primarily for six year olds and four and five year olds in special need. Attendance is part time and charges vary; most centres are run by local authorities, but subsidies are paid to privately run schools.

In 1972 there were 105,000 children in these schools, about 30 per cent of the four to six year olds. Children of working parents who need full-time care are looked after in day nurseries or family day nurseries (individuals who take children into their homes). In 1972 there were 52,000 children (about 6 per cent of the children aged up to six) in day nurseries, the majority of which were publicly provided, though again private nurseries are eligible for subsidy. Another 5 per cent of children up to seven years were in municipal family day nurseries subsidised by the state. In these the minder is employed by the municipality and the establishment must reach certain standards. Other children are looked after by private daily minders.

Sweden now has a target of 90,000 day nursery places by 1975 which should provide for 34 per cent of the expected demand. In assessing demand they took into account mothers working at least half time or studying full time, single fathers, and those with special needs. Another target was to provide general pre-school education for all six year olds for three hours a day by 1975, then to start on five year olds. Other aims are to increase facilities in the smaller towns and rural areas which tend to be worst off, and to ensure that pre-school provision is made in new residential developments above a certain size.

Conclusions

All these countries have various combinations of pre-school facilities which have grown up over several decades in response to social and economic pressures which have been formed by attitudes to children and families. As in this country, the usual pattern is a mixture of day nurseries or creches for younger children, paid for by parents to some extent, and nursery schooling for two to three year olds upwards, which can be free or cost very little. All countries also have individual day care under proper supervision from responsible supervisors. One of the main differences, however, is the acceptance in Europe, both in policy and provision, of the needs of working women with children under, and of, school age. Full day care, for instance, is much more extensive, and several countries have very ambitious plans for this kind of provision, even for very young children.

Another interesting difference is the length of time children spend at nursery school. In the UK and Scandinavia, children spend only a very short time at school, usually only two or three hours, and not every day, whereas in some other countries, once a child starts nursery school it is assumed he will be there all day, possibly from quite early in the morning until the evening if his parents work. This applies even to two year old children, especially in France and Belgium.

Unlike Britain, many countries provide extensive public support through grants and subsidies for privately and voluntarily organised care and education of pre-school children, often to the same level as that provided for state or municipally controlled establishments. There is no rigid distinction between the public and the voluntary sector which are both taken into account when considering demand, supply and finance.

All the countries, except Sweden which has really begun to change the system, divide financial and administrative responsibility between education and health or social services or the equivalent, and most of them are deeply concerned about the lack of coordination and disparities in policy and provision that this causes.

Out of this emerge three generalisations. (1) Whatever is provided in the way of care and education outside the home is eagerly taken up, so that no country has yet reached saturation point. (2) The greatest area of demand and corresponding lack of provision at present, is care for very young children; and all countries, with the exception of the Netherlands and ourselves, have accepted this responsibility and are planning to expand provision substantially. (3) Provision is expensive, especially for very young children, and cannot be looked at only in terms of cash costs, but as part of the labour and family policy as a whole.

In this chapter and the next we discuss controversial questions concerning women with young children who are also in paid employment. As we have seen, the numbers of such mothers both in Britain and in other industrial countries have risen rapidly in recent years and are likely to continue to rise unless the economic situation worsens beyond the worst predictions.

The controversy over whether or not women with young children ought to go out to work, leaving them to be cared for by someone else, usually centres around the issue of whether or not the children suffer if they are not with their mothers nearly all the time. But it raises other issues, which have to do with the role and status of women, and the division of parental roles within the family. We do not for example, question the desirability, and the consequences for their families, of fathers working long hours — and the phrase 'sending his wife out to work' carries the very strong implication that if the wife works but the husband does not (if it is the man and not the woman who stays home and looks after the children) he must be a feeble sort of person.

Today, however, in much of Western Europe, governments have come to accept that many women with young children are in fact working, and that consequently their children are looked after by other people during the day. And they have seen it as a public responsibility to provide services, directly or through subsidised voluntary agencies, to ensure that these young children are properly cared for. But they have gone further than this. They have abandoned the notion that day care services should be made available only for children in special need, and are moving to a situation in which, as in France, services are provided for substantial numbers of infants and one year olds, for as many as one-quarter of all two year olds, and for pretty well all children from the age of three. In Britain we have not done this. Government has vacillated, and public policy has been muddled and hesitating.

We think that the question whether mothers should be employed or stay at home is not, and cannot be, a very fruitful one. Being employed or staying at home can be equally harmful or beneficial to mother and children. So much depends on the family, on the nature and duration of the employment, on the conditions under which the children are cared for by the mother and by those who look after them at other times, and on the degree and quality of support and help they receive, that one cannot generalise. The question is wrongly posed.

In this chapter we present some of the data on which any discussion of employed mothers should draw. In Chapter 8 we discuss attitudes taken by successive governments to employed mothers, we inquire into why it is that mothers are going out to work, and we summarise what we know about the effects of this on the mothers themselves. The effects on children of having mothers at work are considered in Chapter 9 within the context of the general question of the effects on young children of separation from their mothers, due to employment or for any other reason.

In Britain in 1971 there were nearly 590,000 mothers of pre-school children in paid employment, with a further 48,500 seeking paid work, waiting to start a new job or employed but off sick. This means that for every 1,000 mothers with young children, 187 were employed and a further 15 economically active but 'out of employment'.

Of these mothers with under-fives about 176,000 were employed over 30 hours a week, effectively full-time work. (Unless otherwise stated, all information given in this section about Britain is taken from the 10 per cent sample tables of the 1961 and 1971 censuses.) Unfortunately we cannot tell from the census tables how many children under five these working mothers have, since no one in government apparently thought it important to know this. An informed guess is that there are 1.29 children under five for each working mother, making a total of about 821,000 pre-school children with working mothers. (The average for all mothers, working or not, is 1.38 children under five, and this has been reduced by 6 per cent because, overall, working mothers with dependent children of all ages have 6 per cent fewer children than mothers as a whole.) On these figures there are nearly a quarter of a million children under five whose mothers work full-time.

Growth in numbers of working mothers

Going out to work while bringing up a family is becoming increasingly common. Over the decade 1961/71, the proportion of mothers of young children in paid employment increased by 63 per cent (from 115 to 187 per 1,000), the actual numbers employed rising by just under a quarter of a million. In the same decade, the numbers economically active but temporarily out of employment rose even faster, increasing nearly five-fold.

Figure 8 compares the British increase in employment rates for mothers with pre-school age children with those for four other countries for which data are available; it also shows recent employment rates in two other countries. The British increase in the 1960s was greater than for Germany or the United States, but far less than for Sweden, assuming even a small increase there before 1967. However in 1971 the British employment rate was still well below that in Germany, Sweden and the United States, and slightly behind Austria's and Switzerland's. It was only higher than the Netherlands, though the low Dutch rate is in part due to being based only on mothers of children under four. The Netherlands has traditionally had very low economic activity rates for married women, although the number of married women in employment rose over 180 per cent between 1960 and 1971. By comparison, in France, a country with a long tradition of working mothers, the number of employed mothers with at least one child under three rose by over 40 per cent between 1962 and 1968, to 400,000, and it is estimated that this total will have doubled by 1975 (OECD, 1974).

This increase in employment rates for mothers of young children, both in Britain and abroad, is part of a general increase of employment rates for all married women, which has been described in Chapter 1. However the rate of increase

124

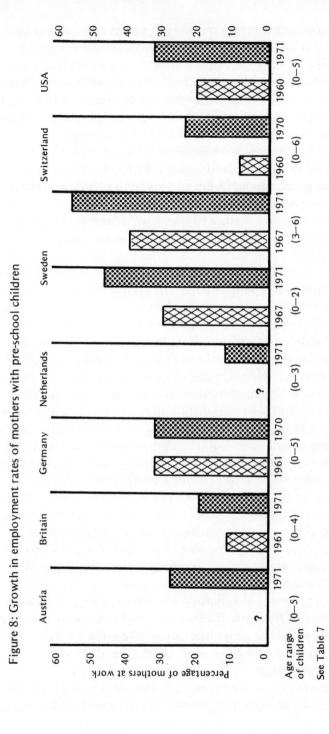

Figure 8: Growth in employment rates of mothers with pre-school children

See Table 7

125

in employment rates for mothers of young children has been faster than for all married women under 60 (63 per cent compared to 42 per cent).

Changes in census practice make it impossible to be certain about how the increase in numbers of employed mothers with young children in Britain in the 1960s varied according to hours worked, but it is likely that the rise amongst part-time workers (those employed less than 30 hours a week) was considerably greater than for full-timers. This would be in line with the general trend in the employment of women since the 1950s which has been marked by 'a large number of women [coming forward for work] taking part-time jobs, the proportion working part-time steadily rising' (Central Statistical Office, 1973).

A number of indicators suggest that the employment rate of mothers with young children has continued to rise since 1971, and that it will carry on rising.

(1) Between June 1971 and June 1975, the number of women employees in Great Britain rose by 734,000 (9 per cent), while the number of male employees fell by 251,000 (*Department of Employment Gazette*, November 1975). As women with young children played a leading part in the increase in female employment during the 1960s, there seems no reason to believe that this is not continuing, especially as the employment rate of older married women aged 35 to 59, which escalated faster than that of any other age group after the war, showed signs of slowing down between 1966 and 1971. One suggested reason for this (*Department of Employment Gazette*, January 1974) is that their maximum employment level is now being reached. With limited reserves of male employees and decreasing reserves of older, married women, the importance of younger married women to the labour force will continue to rise.

(2) Department of Employment forecasts suggest that the major part of the potential increase in labour supply over the next few years will come from women looking for part-time work, a group in which young mothers are likely to be highly represented.

(3) Several local studies in 1973 and 1974 of mothers with young children suggest economic activity rates that are

126

considerably above those in the Census. A sample survey of 600 mothers living in Westminster in 1974 (Westminster Social Services Department, 1975, unpublished) found 42 per cent of mothers employed, 17 per cent of all survey mothers working over 30 hours a week. Another sample survey of part of neighbouring Camden (Thomas Coram Research Unit, 1975, unpublished) showed a very similar proportion (45 per cent) as being employed. A 1973 survey of nearly 1,000 mothers of three and a half year olds, living in the South West and Glamorgan, areas traditionally of low female employment levels, had 3 out of 10 working (University of Bristol, 1974, unpublished).

(4) One factor, especially marked since 1971, which may account for some of the rising numbers of young mothers in employment, is inflation — a second family income being one way of keeping up with, if not ahead of, rising prices. Although the growing numbers of girls who receive higher education or vocational qualifications is likely to lead to an increase in the number of women employed in skilled and rewarding occupations, mothers, and particularly those with young children, do more part-time paid work than other women (70 per cent compared with 42 per cent of married women without children) and are especially likely to be found in unskilled work (though there are no precise figures). These women are also likely to be the main victims of the 'feminising of low-skill occupations', as men move out of them into more skilled work, a movement for which there is now some evidence (Oakley, 1974a).

Although this is the overall picture, employment rates among mothers of young children vary, often considerably, in relation to a number of factors.

Regional differences

Figure 9 shows the variations between some local authorities, those in the Greater London area and the six largest pre-1973 English County Boroughs.

In London, the employment rate for mothers of young children in the Inner London boroughs is 40 per cent above that in Outer London, though three intermediate boroughs, Brent, Ealing and Haringey, which fall in location and

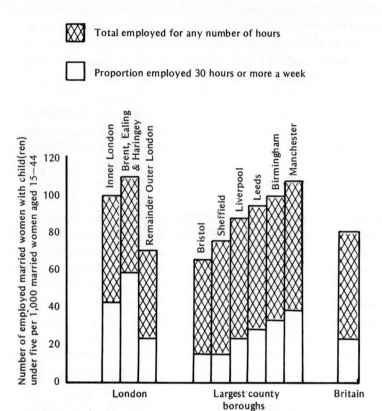

Figure 9: Employment rates for mothers of pre-school children in various local authority areas

Total employed for any number of hours

Proportion employed 30 hours or more a week

See Table 8

128

character between Inner and Outer London, have the highest rates of all. Also more than half the employed mothers in these three boroughs work over 30 hours a week, substantially more than in any of the other areas shown. Considerable variations are also apparent in the six large county boroughs, Manchester at one extreme having an employment rate nearly two thirds greater than Bristol's, and a full-time rate that is more than double.

Variations in employment levels for women, and therefore presumably for mothers with young children, are also found between different types of area. In Klein's study (1965) the percentage of married women in full-time employment was lowest in rural districts and highest in towns of 50,000– 250,000 population, while for part-time work 'small towns offer somewhat fewer opportunities for married women than either rural districts or big cities.' The Government Social Survey study (1968), which included all women, found highest employment rates in conurbations, followed by 'other urban' and, finally, 'rural areas'. A similar pattern where employment is roughly associated with the degree of urbanisation, has been reported from the United States (1971 United States Census). Here the proportion of women aged sixteen and over in the labour force in 1970 was 43 per cent for 'urban' areas, 37 per cent for 'rural non-farm' areas and 32 per cent for 'rural farm' areas.

Marital status

Marital status is one of the most significant factors determining whether the mother of a young child is in full-time employment or not. Separated, widowed, divorced and unmarried mothers are three times more likely to be working full-time (over 30 hours a week) than married mothers living with their husbands (148 per 1,000 compared to 51 per 1,000). Husbandless mothers are also more than three times as likely to be economically active but out of employment. Combining this latter category with those actually 'in employment', 315 husbandless mothers per 1,000 are found to be economically active, nearly 62 per cent more than for other mothers of pre-school children.

However, husbandless mothers only account for 8 per cent of all employed mothers of pre-school children, and 15 per

129

cent of all such mothers working over 30 hours a week. Thus, although the rapidly rising number of one-parent families has contributed to the general rise in the numbers of employed mothers, their contribution to the total has been relatively small. Indeed, between 1961 and 1971 the employment rate of divorced, widowed and single mothers with a child under five actually fell by 23 per cent, whereas that for all married mothers (including those separated from their husbands) rose by 60 per cent. This still meant a doubling in the *numbers* of divorced, widowed and single mothers working (because the total numbers in this group rose by 260 per cent in the decade) but the proportion of *all* employed mothers of young children made up by this group only rose from 3.6 per cent to 4.6 per cent. (Separated but still-married wives are not included in the one-parent group above, because separate information on their employment is not given in the 1961 Census volumes; in 1971 they constituted 48 per cent of all employed mothers of young children not living with a husband.)

Because the numbers of mothers in one-parent families are increasing faster than those in two-parent families, and because they are more likely to be in employment than mothers living with their husbands, their proportion of all employed mothers will continue to increase. But this should not blind us to the fact that the great majority of employed mothers, whether working full or part-time, are both married and in two-parent families.

Social class and education

The stereotype of the employed mother still sets her in the working-class, both by her husband's occupation and the job she does. But Nye and Hoffman (1963), reviewing American experience up to the early 1960s conclude that

the stereotype has persisted but the reality has changed in the post-war era, particularly as American society enters the 1960s. Before the 1940s, the stereotype was close to the facts, the bulk of working mothers (often being the sole support for families of unemployed men) being from the bottom socio-economic strata. But since the war, there has been a trend of maternal employment upwards into the middle-class family, associated with better educated mothers moving into the labour force. Present data indicates the employed mother to be better educated generally than those not employed.

It is impossible to try and trace a similar upward class movement amongst employed mothers in Britain owing to lack of data. The only available data using a national random sample (Government Social Survey 1968) on the social class of employed mothers with young children has numbers that are too small to give much confidence in generalising results; it is also now ten years old. Employment rates were slightly higher amongst mothers with husbands in manual occupations than amongst those with husbands in non-manual occupations. Within these two broad social groups, however, wives of managerial/professional class husbands had higher work rates than wives of 'skilled, non-manual husbands', while among the manual group, wives of semi-skilled workers had the highest rates and wives of 'unskilled, manual husbands', the lowest rates. In a more recent study of a small socially mixed area of London, married mothers with professional or managerial class husbands had higher employment rates (51 per cent) than mothers with manual class husbands (43 per cent) (Thomas Coram Research Unit, 1975, unpublished).

Better documented is the relationship between final levels of education (which is likely to be strongly correlated with social class) and employment rates, the important factor here being experience of further or higher education. Klein (1965) summarises various American investigations as showing 'that the more highly educated or professionally trained a woman is, the more likely she is to have a paid job after marriage'. Similar conclusions come from Europe. In Sweden the proportion of women aged twenty-five to sixty-four who are employed rises steadily according to the level of education received; women with 'post-gymnasium' education have employment rates of 72 to 84 per cent, while for those with less than nine years schooling the rate is only 54 per cent (Swedish Joint Female Labour Council, 1973). In Germany it seems that the most highly skilled and best educated women resume work soonest after having a family, while in France there are indications that between 1963 and 1968 more women were staying on in employment in the years in which they would normally have babies, 'as a result of the considerable improvements in girls' educational levels' (Commission of the European Communities, 1974). In reviewing factors affecting resumption of employment by women, this European report says of educational level: 'the higher this is, the shorter the period away from work.'

In Eastern Europe 'the tendency to remain in the work force or to come back to it after the birth of a child is particularly marked among people who have higher qualifications or who come from a professional or other white-collar background' (Fogarty, Rapoport and Rapoport, 1971). The influence of education on employment among mothers with young children is particularly well illustrated from Hungarian experience. In 1967 new child-care allowances were introduced for mothers with children under three who chose to stay at home to care for them rather than go out to paid work. A study of the first two years of the allowance (Szabady, 1972) shows differences in the rate of use of the allowance according to class and education. The majority of women previously working manually or clerically chose to take the allowance and stay at home, but for better paid and qualified non-manual workers the 'take up' rate was lower.

> The specific choice of non-manual stratum with higher qualifications can be clearly seen by the data broken down according to the level of schooling — those with only general school education made use of the allowance at the rate of 72—73 per cent; for those with secondary school education it was 60—61 per cent; and of the university graduates only 30 per cent temporarily gave up their jobs.

In England, such evidence as there is confirms a partial relationship between educational level and employment rates among mothers of young children. Figure 10 shows the proportion of mothers with children under five employed, according to terminal education age (Government Social Survey, 1968).

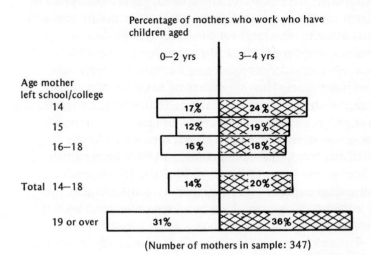

Figure 10: Employment rates of mothers with young children
according to terminal education age

Percentage of mothers who work who have
children aged

	0—2 yrs	3—4 yrs
Age mother left school/college 14	17%	24 %
15	12%	19%
16—18	16%	18%
Total 14—18	14%	20%
19 or over	31%	36%

(Number of mothers in sample: 347)

The mothers with the highest employment rates are those who continued their education to nineteen or over, their rates being much higher than those for all other mothers combined (though the small numbers in the sample for the former group merit caution). The rates for the other groups do not vary markedly, and do not show any tendency to rise with terminal education age, mothers leaving at fourteen or under having rather higher rates than those leaving between fifteen and eighteen. A higher employment rate following further education was found in an earlier comparison of graduate and non-graduate married women aged thirty-five to fifty-five, 55 per cent of the former being employed in 1963 compared to 42 per cent of the latter (Klein, 1965). The difference is smaller than expected but may be due to the inclusion in the non-graduate group of women with other professional training such as teachers.

Age of children

Employment rates for mothers increase as the age of their pre-school children rises, and especially after they pass the age of three. In the Government Social Survey study, the rates for mothers of children over three were over a third greater than for mothers of under-threes, while a similar difference can be seen in the rates given for Sweden in Figure 8. More recently, the study of 600 young mothers in Westminster in 1974 (Westminster Social Services Department 1975, unpublished) showed that whereas a third with children under three were employed, the rate for mothers of children over three was almost a half (49 per cent). This rise in numbers as the child's age increases no doubt reflects current views about the ages at which children can be left, as well as the greater availability of pre-school provision for over threes.

Culture and historical tradition

Finally, culture and historical tradition play a part in influencing employment levels among mothers. Some areas of Britain have histories of high female employment rates (see Chapter 2) associated with the development and needs of a particular industry and often maintained by new industries entering these areas. Perhaps the clearest example of this is found in Lancashire where some textile districts (particularly the Calder Valley and the South East) have traditionally high employment rates for women. Day-care provision is also relatively high, the geographical county of Lancashire having nearly a third of all full-time nursery places provided on factory premises in England and Wales and nearly a quarter of all local authority day nursery places (Department of Health, 1973).

Another instance of this cultural-historical factor is the high employment rate among West Indian mothers. Hood et al (1970) in a sample of 101 West Indian mothers of one year olds living in Paddington, found 51 working, most in full-time and unskilled work. These mothers had been brought up 'with the idea that women worked whenever employment was available [and] many gave the possibility of employment as their main reason for coming to this country'. In another study of a sample of mothers of three year olds in Brixton (Pollak, 1972) 64 per cent of West Indian mothers were employed compared to 37 per cent of English mothers; and the West Indian mothers were five times more likely to work more than four hours a day (51 per cent compared to 11 per cent).

There are no data giving mothers' activity rates separately for other non-white groups, though a recent analysis of 1971 Census data for four cities with different ethnic group composition shows remarkably high employment rates among all non-white mothers taken together (Lomas, 1975), which leave little doubt that the situation of Asian women is becoming similar to that of West Indians. Estimates of activity rates (the percentages of the particular groups under consideration who are working) among non-white mothers of pre-school children were 85 per cent in Leicester, 71 per cent in Manchester, 44 per cent in Bradford and 41 per cent in Wolverhampton. These mothers were also much more likely to be working over 30 hours a week, the proportions for all four cities ranging from 68 to 87 per cent, compared to proportions among white, employed mothers of 24 to 32 per cent.

Although cultural factors play some part in high activity rates among West Indian mothers, the high rates among other non-white groups show clearly that these factors should not be over-stressed. More important and relevant are the severe economic, housing and other pressures facing most non-white families, due to their deprived and unequal position in our society; in all four cities referred to above, for instance, non-white men were more likely to be in unskilled, and therefore worse paid, jobs than white male workers.

The care of young children of employed mothers

A subject of concern, both to the authors of this book, and we hope to the government and public, is how the pre-school children of employed mothers are cared for. It is therefore remarkable that, apart from the results of a few small samples, there is no such information available. Such small studies as there are point to 'the preponderance of individual care over group care' — in short, it is to grannies, husbands and other relatives that most employed mothers look for help rather than institutional forms of care or even paid child-minders. The most recent and extensive survey of employed women (Government Social Survey, 1968) only included a sample of 334 mothers of pre-school children. In these families, husbands (especially where mother worked full-time) provided the necessary care for the majority of pre-school children. Institutional care provided for less than one in six of the children. Between 10 and 20 per cent of the children had mothers who worked at home. We know little about who they are or what they do, but they presumably vary from freelance professionals to machinists involved in sweated labour. Nor do we know much about the effects of such home work on child-care routines and organisation.

A study of 1,000 mothers of three and a half year olds in the South West and Glamorgan (University of Bristol, 1974, unpublished) found that as many as 44 per cent of the children were looked after by their fathers during the mother's 'absence':

the high proportion of children looked after by their father whilst the mother works is interesting and important. This fact alone suggests that a high proportion of mothers who need or wish to go out to work must work

136

during periods when the father is home to look after the children, i.e. evenings, weekends, sometimes overnight. This clearly puts strains on the family.

How far these patterns of child care reflect parents' preferences as opposed to shortages of good, convenient institutional care is an open question. A 1972 study in the Halmstad region of Sweden found that whereas only 9 per cent of employed mothers used day nurseries, 48 per cent would prefer their children cared for in this way, while less than half of the 24 per cent of mothers using relatives considered this a preferred method of care (Swedish Joint Female Labour Council, 1973). Whether or not these results are relevant for Britain, the shortage of institutional care, the frequently inconvenient hours (as with nursery schools) or over-long journeys must play some part in determining current patterns of care (and indeed employment rates) especially for mothers employed full-time.

Some attempt can be made to estimate the shortage of institutional care. The 1971 census figures for mothers with pre-school children, working over thirty hours a week, in England and Wales, give an estimated 205,000 children who need looking after during the day. Matched against this 1971 figure, which, as already explained, may well have increased considerably, there was in 1973 (Department of Health and Social Security, 1973) the following legal day care provision in England and Wales:

Local Authority day nurseries	23,838 places;
Registered private/voluntary premises providing all-day care (ie. private, voluntary and factory nurseries)	25,247 children permitted
Registered day minders providing full-time care	57,042 children permitted
TOTAL	106,127

The shortfall, if local authority provision alone is considered, is enormous. Furthermore it must be remembered that a proportion of places in day nurseries are occupied by children of non-employed or part-time employed mothers and that places are virtually unobtainable for employed married mothers.

Even if legal private and voluntary provision is added in the shortfall remains substantial as is the size of the gap to be filled by relatives, friends and illegal child-minders. The only conclusion to be drawn from this muddled and poorly documented area of need and provision is that the vast majority of day care is provided privately, mostly in the homes of relations and by minders.

Nursery provision and the employment of mothers

Most non-employed mothers of young children expect to resume work at some stage in the future. In the mid-1960s, about half the mothers of pre-school children in the Government Social Survey study (1968) were 'practically certain' or 'likely' to resume work, a fifth were uncertain and only a third rated themselves 'unlikely' to return. More recent studies, in Lancashire and London, report more than four-fifths of mothers of young children wanting to go back to work at some stage, with over half in the more recent study wanting to go back before their youngest child was five (Moss, Tizard and Crook, 1973; Thomas Coram Research Unit, 1975, unpublished).

But how many mothers would seek employment while their children were under five if more places were available in convenient day-care centres? An actual increase in such provision may act as a further spur to demand and increase the number of mothers prepared to contemplate going out to work. This stimulating effect of further provision helps explain why 'in countries where large-scale pre-school provisions are already available, only very few children seem to attend part-time. Unless restrictive measures are taken, the existence of pre-school provision tends to attract more children full-time than might be expected on the basis of need' (OECD, 1973).

In Britain there is considerable evidence that more mothers would go back to work if provision for their pre-school children were available. In the 1973 General Household Survey (Office of Population Censuses and Surveys, 1973) of

138

1,076 women with pre-school children who intended returning to employment, just under two-fifths said they would work earlier if satisfactory arrangements were made for their children. And of 268 mothers in an earlier survey (Government Social Survey, 1968) who said they would probably go back to work and who knew of no pre-school facilities in their neighbourhood, 45 per cent reported they would go back to work sooner if such facilities were available; 52 per cent were undecided and only 7 per cent gave a definite 'no'. The problem of assessing work intentions, and weighing the influence on these of the presence of better services, can be further illustrated from the last study. Out of 689 mothers aged sixteen to twenty-nine with children under sixteen, 297 said they would probably not go back to employment, but in answer to a subsequent question over a quarter of this latter group said they would go back if there were various child-care facilities available.

Lack of adequate pre-school provision, objections of husbands and other household constraints, guilt feelings generated by society's ambivalent feelings towards employed mothers, the lack of work preparation and training of many women, all make it virtually impossible to determine how many mothers would want to go out to paid work if freed of all these constraints. Any realistic assessment of attitudes to employment among mothers requires, at the least, intensive and extensive discussion with mothers; existing studies which have usually relied on a few, crude questions, fail badly on these criteria. But such studies as there have been suggest that the vast majority of mothers of young children want to resume work at some time, and that more say they would return earlier if there were more and better pre-school provision. The rapidly rising number of mothers going to work in recent years and the very high activity rates in more advanced economies like Sweden and America (see Figure 8) confirm this impression and reinforce the need to look at future pre-school provision in the context of rising employment trends.

Manpower implications of trends in employment
At a time when unemployment is reaching its highest level since the second world war, and rising, it may seem

particularly fatuous to ask whether an increase in nursery services would be likely to lead to a net increase in the labour force. However if demand for labour increases in the long-term, as projected (partly because of a reduction in working hours), will nursery services on a large scale be able to recruit enough staff and still release additional women for the general labour market?

Doubts about the value to the labour force of the day nursery programme were increasingly voiced during the second world war when the actual results of expansion came to be looked at. In 1943 the Committee of Public Accounts concluded that the additional number of women who were working in industry as a result of nursery provision was 'disappointingly small' and that the nursery expansion involved a disproportionate cost. It found that 16,688 women were employed in day nurseries to care for 45,244 children — 2.7 children per staff member — and released an estimated 38,829 mothers for full-time employment. A further study of Birmingham day nurseries in 1945 showed that 948 full-time-equivalent staff (3.7 per child including non child-care workers) released 2,784 mothers for full-time work and a further 359 for part-time employment (or 3.3 mothers released to employment for every day nursery worker).

These figures and conclusions need some qualifying in present day circumstances. In 1973, there were approximately 3.7 children on day nursery registers for every full-time-equivalent member of staff, counting all nursery students as full-time workers and assuming ancillary staff to be equivalent to 20 per cent of the child-care workers. Although this figure is comparable with that in Birmingham, it differs considerably from the national 1943 staff:child ratio, the lower ratio implying a higher potential net labour gain in 1973. The reason for this difference is that in the wartime nurseries there were more children aged under two; and such children need staffing levels roughly twice those needed by the over-twos. The net labour gain from day nurseries at current staff rates, could thus be substantial, especially for women with children over the age of two.

Crude labour gain calculations assume a uniformity among women, in terms of experience, expertise, training and natural talents. In practice, mothers released into employment, and nursery staff taken on to care for their children, tend to have different skills: a day nursery worker, with particular talents for work with young children, may, for example, release into employment a nurse and shorthand typist. Day nurseries did make some contribution to this improved 'job fit' in the war:

> in the textile areas and in some other skilled occupations, there is little doubt that young married women, valuable because of previous training, were able to return to their old jobs, and that nursery workers could in no sense have been substitutes for them in industry (Ferguson and Fitzgerald, 1954).

Conclusion

An increase in pre-school services is advocated throughout this book, and is in part already accepted by government, for reasons other than the needs of the economy. Even the case for increased help to employed mothers is based first on widening the choices open to women and improving the facilities available to them and their children. But the increase in all the pre-school services will obviously involve a considerable increase in numbers employed in them, though less proportionately for services open for shorter hours than day nurseries. The creation of new jobs, in a labour-intensive occupation, in the context of increasing the wellbeing of large numbers of parents and children, seems to us a perfectly acceptable proposition in the last quarter of the twentieth century — indeed it has been generally acceptable in the public health, welfare and education services for many years. A likely result of increasing the number of nursery places is that more women will seek employment in industry and elsewhere than will be required to staff the nurseries. It cannot be said therefore that there are not enough people available to staff a comprehensive nursery service and do all the other work society wants done.

Mothers who do paid work, especially those with pre-school children, are a constant source of controversy, and are subject to strong and often dogmatic censure. The Plowden Committee for instance (Central Advisory Council, 1967) was moved to 'deplore the increasing tendency of mothers of young children to work'. A more recent government document on preparing people for parenthood (Department of Health, 1974a) summarised the views of a number of professional, voluntary and research organisations, and noted that 'a strong theme to emerge from the consultations [with these organisations] was that mothers of young children in particular should be encouraged to stay at home.' Particular attention was given to the views of one research body, that 'society in. general and women in particular should be helped to appreciate that staying at home with their children was not a waste of their education and talents, but such a worthwhile and challenging task that it justified their devoting practically undivided attention to providing a secure yet stimulating environment for their children, at least for the first two to three years.' In addition, 'a range of medical and nursing opinion was in favour of efforts to dissuade mothers from going out to work'.

The attitude of governments, irrespective of party, to employed mothers has been in general to discourage them, not through any explicit and elaborated policy, but through failing to provide services geared to the needs of these mothers and neglecting even to discuss these needs. The main exception to this rule, apart from attempts to attract married teachers and nurses back to employment, has been unsupported mothers who are specifically included as a priority group for day nursery admissions (see Ministry of Health circular 37/68), though even for this group the actual provision is inadequate.

Moreover, despite a 63 per cent increase in the 1960s in the proportion of mothers with young children at work, government documents shaping developments in pre-school provision ignore the subject and the issues it raises. The 1972 Education White Paper (Department of Education, 1972) which initiated the current expansion of nursery education, and the subsequent circular (Department of Education circular 2/73) which discussed the implementation of this new nursery policy, manage to make *no* mention of employed mothers. Even more remarkable is the silence on the whole matter in government planning for day nursery expansion. When talking about day care for children in the circular on ten-year development plans for social services departments (Department of Health circular 35/72) the Department of Health also makes no reference to employed mothers, even those who are unsupported. The low target of 8 day nursery places per 1,000 children under five, shows clearly that it is not envisaged that day nurseries will play a significantly larger role than at present in the care of children of employed mothers.

An attempt to grapple with the whole problem of employed mothers and pre-school provision was made by the Plowden Committee, and the muddle they got into illustrates the dilemmas, contradictions and controversy pervading the whole debate. The Committee basically 'deplored' employed mothers, but accepted that they produced 'economic yields', would be a source of staff for nursery expansion, and that their increasing numbers reflected the effects of important economic trends. They also believed firmly that nursery expansion should be basically part-time because 'our evidence is that it is generally undesirable, except to prevent a greater evil, to separate mother and child for a whole day in a nursery'. In the case of employed mothers with 'financial need' (undefined), some responsibility for their children within an expanded nursery service seems to be accepted, and children of full-time working mothers are one of the groups for whom the 15 per cent of full-time nursery school places is planned. But these places are acknowledged to be only part of the answer, for 'a full-time working mother must expect her·child will attend a nursery for extended hours and during school holidays.'

This crucial point having been made, there is no further discussion in the Plowden Report of its implications for services. The careful reader is left to assume that provision for these children will be in the large nursery and children's centres discussed in an earlier paragraph. This however, makes no attempt to discuss the size of the need or the problems of organising holiday and all-day care in such centres.

Plowden also makes no reference to mothers employed part-time and how nursery provision could or should help them; and it dismisses full-time employment 'where mothers are not obliged to work' as undesirable and not to be encouraged by making provision for their children: 'it is no business of the educational service to encourage these mothers'. Finally it recognises, but does no more, one obvious consequence of such a restricted service: 'it is true, unfortunately, that the refusal of full-time nursery places for these children may prompt some [of the mothers] to make unsuitable arrangements for their children's care'.

A year later, the Seebohm Report (Committee on Local Authority and Allied Personal Social Services, 1968) also considered services for the under-fives. It noted society's ambivalent attitude to working mothers, and reflected this ambivalence in its own conclusions. While stating that 'it is detrimental to the child to be separated from its mother for long periods during early childhood,' the Report acknow-ledged that mothers will continue to go out to work, that many children were being looked after in unsatisfactory conditions, that services were inadequate and that a clear national policy was needed. There the argument ends, and the Report returns to discussing how various combinations of nursery education, playgroups and day nurseries could cater for those mothers and children who suffer from particular disadvantages and stresses. The 1974 Finer Committee Report on One-Parent Families also discusses the issue, but in relation only to single-parent families, which constitute only 8 per cent of families with an employed mother of a child or children under five.

What happens to the young children of employed mothers seems, then, not to be the official concern of anyone, and this indifference is reflected in the shortage of public day-care provision. Where attempts have been made to justify the failure to provide day-care services, some anonymous body of professional opinion is referred to, rather than any discussion of the evidence. Attention is paid to some unargued (and indeed contentious) statement of what should be, according to the opinion drawn on, rather than to what is actually happening and what is required to respond to real-life trends and needs:

> day care must be looked at in relation to the view of medical and other authority that early and prolonged separation from the mother is detrimental to the child; wherever possible the younger pre-school child should be at home with his mother; and the needs of older pre-school children should be met by part-time attendance at nursery schools or classes (Department of Health circular 37/68).

or again:

> the majority of educationalists regard part-time attendance at school as sufficient, indeed preferable, for most children until they reach compulsory school age (Department of Education, 1972).

Clearly the implied reasoning in all this is that, if services are not provided, then mothers will be obliged to stay at home and enjoy their proper role as mother and wife. The main result, is, however, that many working mothers have to make child-care arrangements that are not satisfactory for them or their children; they feel guilty and their children may suffer, fulfilling too often the expectation that it is a bad thing for mothers of young children to go to work.

Why do mothers work?

The motivation for, and consequences of, mothers working have not been studied much. Since Yudkin's pioneer work (Yudkin and Holme, 1969) few attempts have been made to collate and review existing information and knowledge and identify areas of ignorance, though as Yudkin commented, ignorance of the facts has not prevented ardent controversy. Our knowledge is limited by the superficiality of past studies, most of which have relied on a few, crude questions which have failed to explore in any depth the meaning and satisfaction of women's lives. The following discussion is limited by this unsatisfactory base.

Money and independence

The most common reason given by mothers of young children for going, or wanting to go to work, is money. When attempts have been made to distinguish between money needed for 'genuine necessity' or 'the sheer necessities of life' as opposed to money needed to raise family living standards or for 'wants above the necessity level', 'non-essential' financial needs are found to heavily outnumber the 'essential' ones. This has led one writer (Klein, 1965) to conclude that 'for most married women, irrespective of their class, money appears to be a means of increasing their standard of living, rather than of keeping the wolf from the door.' However, distinctions between 'essential' and 'non-essential' needs are difficult to make and are almost bound to be arbitrary. A satisfactory analysis of the financial motivation of employed mothers can only be made in the context of the financially disadvantaged position of families with young children, both compared to other families and to their own position before they had children.

Recent studies of family living standards show clearly that the incidence of poverty is above average in families with young children, and that they are generally worse off than other families. A report in 1971 (Department of Health, 1971) showed that families with a child under five were more likely to be living below supplementary benefit level than other families. They were also twice as likely to be in the group living just above the 'poverty line' (that is, with resources of £5 or less over supplementary benefit level). The report concludes that this 'is principally because the mother of a family with at least one child under five has a substantially lower probability of earning'. The General

Household Survey (Office of Population Censuses, 1973) also illustrates the comparatively deprived position of families with young children. 71 per cent of households with a youngest child aged five to fifteen had a gross income of more than £30 a week, compared to only 57 per cent of households with a pre-school child. The difference was not so much in the income of the household head, as in *total* household income, probably reflecting the higher incidence of working wives in households without very young children. The arrival of the first child often means the loss of up to half of the family income, and this, with increasing expenditure, represents the steepest decline in a family's cycle of financial fortune. This decline is further exacerbated by the decreasing numbers of men earning their living through physically demanding manual labour, where earnings often peak at an early age when physical powers are at a maximum; now increasingly earnings rise with age, so that having a young family is more likely to coincide with a relatively low income point in a lifetime's work cycle.

Not surprisingly, finance is reported as a more important factor in work motivation among working-class as opposed to middle-class wives. In Klein's study (1965) 43 per cent of employed wives of professional and managerial class husbands mentioned financial reasons for employment, as opposed to 79 per cent of the wives of semi-skilled or unskilled manual workers. In the later Social Survey Study (Governmental Social Survey, 1968) 68 per cent of manual workers' wives, as against 52 per cent of non-manual workers' wives gave 'needing the money' as a reason for probably returning to work. The difference when related to husbands' income was even more marked. 'Needing money' was a factor given by 78 per cent of wives whose husband's income was under £10 a week, but only 48 per cent where income was over £20.

Another financial reason for wives entering employment is to increase their independence, total economic dependency being one of the main features of non-employed wives. This occurs even in homes where income is shared on a more equal basis, such dependence manifesting itself in feelings of guilt for the mother if she spends money on herself — the only money she spends guiltlessly is on food for the family and clothes for the children. Yudkin illustrates this:

147

many of our respondents amplified their answers [about reasons for going out to work] by indicating the use to which extra income was being put. None desired the money for themselves though some frankly admitted that the extra money provides 'jam for the bread'.

A child-care or single-wage allowance

To earn money, either as an addition to the family budget or as a means to greater independence, is obviously a factor influencing mothers − and everyone else − to go out to work. Paying mothers to stay at home to care for their children has therefore been proposed both by those who believe that if mothers work their children suffer, and by those who argue that the present lack of payment for housework and child-care is part of the gross exploitation of women.

In Hungary concern about flagging birth-rates and higher morbidity rates among infants in nurseries led to the introduction of a new child-care allowance in 1967. The allowance is paid to a working woman who opts to stay at home after her baby is born, and it continues for the first three years of the child's life. The allowance increases for each additional child under three looked after at home, the basic allowance for one child being just over a quarter of the basic industrial wage. In France, a 'single-salary allowance' is paid to low-income families with dependent children and only one wage-earner. In both countries, there are also substantial family allowances, well above those paid in Britain which are the lowest in the European Economic Community.

It is significant that both Hungary and France combine their allowances with extensive benefits and services for mothers who still choose to work. Hungary, for instance, with a population less than a fifth of Great Britain's, had 43,000 all-day nursery places for children up to three in 1972 and 234,000 nursery school places, mostly full-time for children between three and six. Working mothers can also take paid leave to care for sick children; are entitled to time off twice daily to breast feed; and are also entitled to the same or a similar job at the same wage on returning to work after drawing their child-care allowances, as well as training and refresher courses.

148

It is difficult to assess the effects of these Hungarian and French allowances. Both are limited in coverage, to low-income families in France and to families with children under three in Hungary. France has a very high employment rate for mothers — with nearly 700,000 mothers with children under three in employment in 1973 — and the employment rate has risen rapidly in recent years despite the allowance. In Hungary, the differential take-up rate between women with differing occupational and educational experience has been described in Chapter 7. However an increasing number of Hungarian mothers are now claiming the benefit, the number having risen from 144,000 in 1970 to 230,000 in 1975. Today three-quarters of women who are eligible take advantage of the benefit after starting their families. But a quarter still continue to work after becoming mothers, while others return to work within three years. The case for a similar child-care or single-wage allowance in Britain raises a number of points. First its effects on the numbers of mothers in employment would depend on how much was offered and on what limits were placed on eligibility for it. In any case, it would probably have a differential class effect, as in Hungary, where only a minority of better-paid mothers in professions and other skilled jobs take it up. Secondly its appeal to mothers would obviously depend on the reasons why they went out to work. As already suggested, though money is an important reason for most people — mothers or not — going out to work, there are other reasons why increasing numbers of mothers want to do so. The results from a recent study of a socially mixed area of London put the importance of money into perspective. Of the 45 per cent of mothers of young children in employment, most gave money as one reason for working. However less than a fifth said they would stop work if money came into the family from another source (Thomas Coram Research Unit, 1975, unpublished).

Any proposal for a new single-wage allowance might best be seen as a measure which increased the choices open to women and to families as a whole. It could allow those mothers — and fathers — who would prefer to devote themselves more to home and children to do so, provided it was set at a high enough level (and to influence full-time

149

workers, this would have to be quite high). It was with this aim, of broadening 'the true scope of choice for the lone mother between staying at home and going out to work', that the Finer Committee suggested the introduction of a guaranteed maintenance allowance for one-parent families. If this principle was extended to any family with dependent children and less than two full-time working adults, more parents could work part-time, deciding the hours they wished to work on domestic rather than financial grounds.

There is another argument for a single-wage allowance which is much wider than its likely effect on the numbers of mothers of young children who seek employment. Today, in Britain most mothers with children under five are *not* employed: their families have therefore only one income and existing state benefits to supplement this are very inadequate. By contrast, in 1971, two-thirds of married couples without dependent children enjoyed two incomes from work. Consequently families with dependent children, are at a considerable financial disadvantage. An allowance paid to households with dependent children, with only one income or, more ambitiously, less than two full-time incomes, would be a major contribution to reducing family poverty and the generally disadvantaged position of families with children.

Professional and vocational reasons

Most existing studies probably under-estimate the current significance of vocational and professional motives for mothers working, having been completed in the mid or early 1960s before the effects of the rapid growth of further education for women would have made itself fully felt. In Yudkin's study, in which middle-class mothers were under-represented, less than 2½ per cent of employed mothers gave 'professional and vocational interest' as their main reason for doing paid work, while in the Social Survey Study (1968) only 3.1 per cent of married women in households with children gave 'interest in specific field of work or to use qualifications' as reasons for resuming work. However, amongst all employed married women who ceased education at nineteen or over, the proportion rose to 21 per cent.

150

Dissatisfaction and depression

Apart from financial and professional/vocational work motives, surveys have reported a variety of other reasons which might be summarised as 'dissatisfaction with non-employed lot'; for example, boredom, need of social stimulation, not enough to do at home, need for companionship, need to get away from home and housework. The high incidence of isolated, unsatisfactory and stressful lives among housewives and especially mothers has been commented on over the years by a number of writers. A report prepared in the first world war concluded that for the average working-class woman 'her day begins, continues and ends with household drudgery, that the claims made on her time by husband and children are unceasing and that the better the mother, the less the leisure' (Women's Cooperative Guild, 1917). A generation later, another report on the health and conditions of working-class wives based on a survey of 1,250 married women 'yields a picture in which monotony, loneliness, discouragement and sordid hard work are the main features — a picture of almost unredeemed drabness. Happiness can suffer an almost unperceived lowering of standard which results in a pathetic gratitude for what might be called negative mercies' (Spring-Rice, 1939).

Another war and generation later, an American review of employment among mothers (Nye and Hoffman, 1965) refers to 'a voice heard here and there that adults are people too and that they have socio-psychological needs which merit consideration in family and action programmes'. Reference is also made to the work of two sociologists, Komorovsky and Landis, both of whom feel 'that for the talented, trained and ambitious woman, the life of the non-employed mother is too limited and monotonous; even if she is untrained and lacks talents and ambitions, she may still find life dull.' Komorovsky (1953) describes two kinds of maternal discontent, some wives being unhappy only with some particular aspect of their housewife role, others reluctantly giving up jobs but yearning to return. She emphasises that even women with no desire for employment show considerable dissatisfaction with the homemaker role. Gavron's study (1966) of 100 mothers of small children also indicated considerable dissatisfaction. Many mothers were bored and lonely at home, and the majority wanted to work: 'a lot of housework is drudgery. Nothing has prepared young wives for the boredom of scrubbing floors and ironing shirts. But on the other hand there is the feeling that being at home is not as important as being at work.'

Most recently, under the influence of the women's liberation movement, not only have the negative aspects of women's housework and child-rearing functions been described and discussed more fully, but they have been related to a more general critique of women's role and place in society. There is a questioning of such basic issues as the existing division of labour by sex, and the validity of the view that the primary child-rearing role must be undertaken by the biological mother. More specific criticisms of the housewife's situation include its economic dependence, the low status and social trivialisation of housework, the isolation and incessant nature of the job, and the reduction of the housewife's role to a point where fulfilment has to be found through servicing and maintaining others.

Three recent studies lend some empirical backing to these views. In the first study, of 40 women with children under five (divided equally between middle and working-class) 70 per cent from each class were rated as being dissatisfied or very dissatisfied with their work as housewives (Oakley, 1974a, 1974b). Monotony, the fragmentation of their work and time pressures — factors often associated with dissatisfaction among industrial workers — were each experienced by over half the housewives, and in each case were more often experienced by housewives than by factory or assembly line workers. As reported in this inquiry, average weekly hours of housework (including child care) were 77, with a range of 48 to 105 hours — a finding consistent with 11 earlier studies from Britain, France and the United States between 1929 and 1971, which suggests that there has been no decline in hours worked despite the advent of various household aids. Oakley estimates that on average one child adds 23 hours a week to housework and two children add 35 hours. This is in line with a Swedish estimate (cited in Wynn, 1970) that each child under two requires an extra 20 hours a week of attention and direct handling. The other two studies of mothers of young children throw light on their vulnerability to depression. This is strikingly apparent in a recent study of psychiatric disturbance in women carried out by Brown (1975). On the basis of an interview schedule developed at the Institute of Psychiatry, London, and the validation of a psychiatrist's clinical diagnosis, 35 out of a random sample of 220 women (16 per cent) were judged to have suffered from a definite psychiatric disorder in the three months up to interview. As well as depressive mood, all of these 35 'reported a cluster of symptoms, such as loss of weight, lack of energy, various forms of sleep disturbance, heightened anxiety and other basically unpleasant experiences which distinguish them from other women.'

The incidence of disturbance in Brown's study varied markedly according to social class and life-stage. Of working-class women, 25 per cent were judged to have had a recent or chronic disturbance as opposed to only 5 per cent of middle-class women. But the group with the highest incidence were working-class mothers with a child under five, 42 per cent of whom had been disturbed, compared to 17 per cent with a youngest child of school age and 5 per cent of middle-class mothers with young children. This very high figure for working-class mothers receives confirmation from another study, looking at the health of children under five on a council housing estate in North London. Using a semi-structured interview, 42 per cent of mothers were assessed as having been clearly psychiatrically disturbed in the previous twelve months, 16 per cent very seriously so (Richman, 1974).

These are profoundly troubling studies. Moreover, it is not just the case that all those mothers, of whatever social class, who are not severely depressed are necessarily problem-free. In Brown's total sample, in addition to the many mothers judged to have suffered a recent psychiatric disorder, a further substantial group were rated as 'borderline' cases, who had definite symptoms, which were however less severe that those of the most disturbed group. When discussing the stresses of young mothers, we are studying a continuum of experience, from those who find their lives fulfilling and happy to those who suffer profound depression, with all sorts of variations and contrasting experiences in between. While many young mothers enjoy their lives, and find satisfaction in them, the numbers whose lives are marked by unhappiness, dissatisfaction and strain are much larger than generally recognised.

One of the measures devised by Brown to explain the high incidence of depression in working-class women was an 'intimacy' scale, the highest score on which applied to a woman considered to have a close, intimate and confiding relationship with husband or boy-friend. The presence of such a relationship was found to be a factor militating against the onset of depression. But Brown found that though

> working-class women start well . . . there is a dramatic change as soon as they have children . . . only 37 per cent with a child under five [have the highest 'intimacy' score], half the proportion of the corresponding middle-class group. Thus working-class women in the early stages of rearing their families are doubly at risk; firstly because they experience more severe events and major difficulties than their middle-class counterparts and secondly because the quality of their marriage at this stage is, on the whole, poor.

Low 'intimacy' does not appear to be a permanent feature of working-class marriage, the quality of marriages improving as children grow older — a hint of the particular strains of young parenthood.

Any attempt to tackle the question of the housewife's and mother's lot is forced to recognise the lack of serious attention paid to it. There are however indications to suggest that the lot of many mothers is unsatisfactory and unsatisfying, even damaging, and that the causes may be inherent in existing family and social norms, roles and structures. The issues involved and their implications seem important enough to merit wider, deeper and more sensitive study and discussion.

The consequences of employment for mothers
It is difficult to get an objective, balanced picture of the consequences for mothers of going out to work. Most studies

154

have concentrated only on some aspects of the effects on children, and to some extent on family relationships. Few consider the mother's experience, the effects on the family of extra resources, or the costs and benefits to the economy and society as a whole. None look at the consequences of high full-time employment rates among fathers or of mothers not being employed.

A working mother is likely to have different ideas about herself and her role in the family, and some studies have looked at the effect on family relationships. Two American studies (cited in Nye and Hoffman, 1963) reported differences favouring the employed mother's attitude towards relationships with her children. Thus for instance, Nye, in a study of 2,000 mothers of school-age children and over 200 mothers of pre-school children, found employed mothers had a more favourable attitude towards children and motherhood (provided they had no more than three children). In considering marital relationships, Nye cautiously suggests that problems associated with maternal employment are more likely to show themselves in the husband-wife relationship than elsewhere. Findings suggest a poorer marital relationship and more conflicts in families with working mothers. However, it is not clear whether employment, with the resulting change in role and power, produces conflict, or whether wives enter employment because they are already dissatisfied with their marital relationships.

Other studies of employed women and marital relationships concentrate on husbands' attitudes to their wives working. In Klein's study (1965), wives tended to overestimate the amount of unconditional approval or disapproval from their husbands, who were more prepared to qualify their answers on this point. The vast majority of husbands however gave at least conditional approval. Very few husbands (4 per cent for part-time and 14 per cent for full-time work) disapproved totally. In Yudkin's sample of employed mothers, 63 per cent believed their husbands did not mind, and realised the need for them to go to work, and a further 25 per cent said their husbands were in full agreement. In the Social Survey study covering married women with and without children (Government Social

Survey, 1968), 14 per cent of those employed said their husbands actively liked or encouraged their employment, while 61 per cent said their husbands did not mind; 17 per cent said their husbands did mind. This study also suggests that the husbands of women who have received further education are more likely to be strongly in favour of their employment.

Apart from self-reports on the pros and cons of employment, we know little about the effects on the mothers themselves of being employed. Undoubtedly combining a job with care of the house and children can be a strain but there is evidence from George Brown's study of depression that employment helps to increase the resistance of mothers to the onset of depressive episodes. Of the women in his sample with a child at home who had experienced a severe event or major difficulty in the preceding year, 44 per cent of the non-employed mothers developed a psychiatric disturbance compared to only 14 per cent of those with a job. A job, he suggests, may be protective, not because it can prevent threatening or other stressful events or difficulties from occurring, but because it helps the mother to cope with them if they do occur. Brown speculates that one reason why factors such as employment or a high 'intimacy' score can be protective may be because they help preserve a woman's self-esteem. Without such protection ' a sense of failure and dissatisfaction [may be generated] in meeting the internalised expectations of being a good mother and wife and this in turn leads to chronically low self-esteem, leaving women particularly vulnerable to the effects of loss.'

This theme of self-esteem appears in the work of Feld (in Nye and Hoffman, 1965), who found high self-esteem more prevalent among employed women, though he also found that more employed women felt inadequate as mothers. Nye suggests that these findings are compatible; employed mothers have higher self-esteem as individuals, but when their work and family commitments conflict, they feel inadequate.

Most married women show a high level of satisfaction in their paid work. In Yudkin's sample, 88 per cent expressed positive enjoyment in their job. Klein posed her question in terms of the differences employment had made to wives' married lives; 59 per cent only mentioned advantages, 27 per cent said it made no difference and only 9 per cent mentioned disadvantages. In his sample of 2,000 mothers, Nye found support for the position that women employed full-time found more satisfaction in their work than non-employed women found in housework. Finally in the 1972 Household Survey more part-time workers, most of whom were women, rated themselves 'very satisfied' with their jobs (64 per cent) than did the mainly male full-timers (50 per cent). Taking all these studies into account, it seems fair to conclude that women show high levels of satisfaction in their employment which, given the unskilled and low status nature of many of their jobs, may well reflect on the satisfactions to be gained from staying at home. The housewives in Oakley's study, irrespective of class 'had a deep-seated, high appreciation of the rewards experienced in outside work, the resultant comparison with housework [branding] it as a less enjoyed and less enjoyable occupation'.

Conclusion

The increasing number of employed mothers is a secular, social and economic trend of major significance the implications of which have been largely ignored by industry, education, welfare and social services. Neglect is most apparent in the lamentable record of care for children under three, where public services have failed in quality and quantity. Faced by this situation, employed mothers have been forced to make private arrangements that are often unsatisfactory. To avoid this state of affairs we need a positive and comprehensive policy to enable women, including those who are mothers, to use their full potential and to share with men, on a basis of equality, the full range of domestic, social and employment experiences.

9 For whom should we provide?

As we have seen, the need, and the modern desire, for educational and day care *services* for young children have arisen out of the changes in the manner in which people have lived over the last two centuries. With the agricultural and industrial revolutions, a society based on small-scale agriculture and domestic industry gave way to modern industrial society. Work, and place of work, came to be no longer centred on the dwelling-place or the surrounding fields. Fathers, and increasingly mothers, went *out* to work — at first taking their children, but later leaving them behind to look after themselves or be cared for by somebody else. In the nineteenth century a sharp distinction was created between the world of childhood and that of adult life, and with this a new set of problems came into being.

For older children, a solution to some of these problems came through the institution of the school. Before the nineteenth century it was not necessary for most children to go to school at all. For those who did, school started at seven or eight — as it still does in some continental countries — and followed prescribed conventional patterns of instruction. These survived almost intact throughout the nineteenth century, and into the twentieth. However, the new industrialism brought new educational needs which were eventually met by the introduction of compulsory 'elementary' schooling, designed to teach the three Rs and a modicum of Christianity to the masses. It was recognised that most children before the age of about six were too young to cope with formal school work. For them, therefore, education seemed a futile undertaking — and the identification of education with literacy was responsible not only for the lack of educational provision for young children, but also for the concept of 'ineducability' which was applied to the mentally retarded who, until 1971, were in England excluded from the educational system.

During the nineteenth century, however, the need for society to intervene in order that young children should be cared for and protected became obvious; and as the century wore on, larger and larger numbers of two, three and four year old children began to crowd into the elementary schools along with their older sibs and neighbours. Since parents, in sending their children to school, gave over to the public authorities the task of providing them with education, the education authority had itself to formulate what the purposes of 'preschool' education were to be, and decide how these were to be achieved. And when, largely in the twentieth century, public responsibility began to be assumed for the day care of some young children, the health and welfare authorities had likewise both to formulate their nursery objectives, and devise administrative structures within which to carry them out. The problem of educating and caring for young children, which had not been seen to exist in the Middle Ages, and which had been placed firmly in the hands of parents until late in the nineteenth century, became increasingly one for the public authorities.

Each public authority charged with the business of providing services for young children went its own way — it still does to a large extent. Residential nurseries operating under the Poor Law became little workhouses, and later, under the Health authorities, little hospitals for children who were not sick. Day nurseries disclaimed educational aims and concerned themselves primarily with matters of health and hygiene, and secondarily with how to 'occupy' the children. And most schools took no responsibility for the wellbeing of children during school holidays, or before or after school.

In planning the downward extension of those services for young children for which they were administratively responsible, the public authorities, at central and local level, tended to ignore completely needs which it was not their statutory responsibility to provide for — and even the services they were 'empowered' but not legally obliged to provide were always starved of resources. Thus in 1933 the Hadow Report on Nursery and Infant Education, though containing many references to the need for nursery schools for the children of working mothers, did not discuss what happened, or what should happen, to the children of these mothers during out-of-school hours, or in school holidays. Likewise the Curtis Committee (1946) which reviewed the needs of 'deprived' children living in institutional care, was prevented by its terms of reference from considering the problems of children living in their own homes in conditions which crippled their development. And though the Plowden Report (1967) on primary education discussed the need for a combined day-care and nursery school service for young children, the responsibility to provide services remained divided, both centrally and locally, between two Departments neither of which has a statutory duty to see that they are adequate to meet the community's needs. In consequence we have yet to provide nursery services for children which give the continuity and consistency of care that everyone agrees are so desirable.

How large should a nursery service be?

One of the great merits of the Plowden Report was that it did address itself to the question of estimating the numbers of places required in a nursery service. The Plowden view, which has by and large been officially accepted (though not by any means fully implemented), was that most children under the age of three are too young to tolerate separation from their mothers. However, alternative care for those who require it should, the Report said, be given in day nurseries. Nursery education, on a part-time basis except for 15 per cent of children in special need, should be available to all children whose parents wish them to attend 'at any time after the beginning of the school year after they reach the age of three'. Children over the age of three in full day care should have education provided either in a nursery class or in a near-by nursery school during school hours.

The Plowden recommendation marked a new step in public acceptance of a duty to provide education for young children. Earlier legislation had *empowered* local authorities to provide for it out of rates and taxes, but they had been discouraged from doing so except for children in poor home circumstances. The Plowden Report however stressed the desirability of nursery provision 'not only on educational grounds but also for social, health and welfare considerations'. The case, the committee believed, was a strong one.

They advanced three main lines of argument. First, they cited with approval the Nursery Schools Association's Memorandum to the Committee as justification for the nursery school. They

> wanted more nursery places because most children can benefit from the physical care, the enriched opportunities for play both indoors and out, the companionship of other children and the presence of understanding adults which nursery education provides. Children need opportunities to get to know people outside their own family circle and to form some relationships which are less close and emotionally charged. The earlier maturity of children increases their need for companionship and stimulus before the age of attendance at school. . . .
>
> Long before a child is five [Plowden went on] he is already using words and is often familiar with books, toys and music. The issue is not whether he should be 'educated' before he reaches school age because that is happening anyway. What has to be decided is whether his education is to take place in increasing association with older children and under the supervision of skilled people, as well as of parents, in the right conditions and with the right equipment.

Plowden's other two arguments related to children in poor home circumstances rather than to the psychological and educational needs of children 'with a stable home background, companionship with their parents and their brothers and sisters, and sufficient space indoors and out'. They pointed out that many children did not enjoy these advantages, and that others were socially deprived or had special handicaps.

There is no dispute today about the need for nursery provision for disadvantaged children. However, for the majority of children, who are not disadvantaged, the case for nursery education requires justification — and the Plowden justification rests on the arguments summarised in the quotation from the Nursery Schools Association Memorandum given above. This case was supported overwhelmingly by the teachers and informed observers whom Plowden consulted.

Only one member of the Plowden Committee, Mrs M. Bannister, entered a note of reservation on nursery education. Mrs Bannister suggested that only in educational priority areas were nursery schools justified. Elsewhere all efforts should be made to provide playgroups and play centres, open all day and throughout the year, staffed largely by mothers but enjoying the help given by a highly trained peripatetic teacher, and catering for younger as well as older children. Mrs Bannister deplored on educational grounds the increase in the numbers of mothers seeking paid employment, since she thought that nursery education, which separated children from their younger sibs and from their parents, was psychologically harmful. She was doubtful about the possibility of nursery schools recruiting, training and holding enough staff of suitable calibre, and thought that taking children from their parents for part of the day would not necessarily do much to help the mothers in their loneliness and boredom. Finally, she said

> It is an open question whether the money which it is proposed to spend on nursery education in 'educational priority areas' might not be better spent on housing. Since all our evidence suggests the quality of the home has the decisive influence on the child's educational future, the money might be better spent on improved housing and means directed towards improving maternal care.

Mrs Bannister's reservations about nursery education were not shared by the informed public at the time. But in the changed economic circumstances of today they are likely to be taken more seriously — if only because in times of financial stringency any excuse to cut public expenditure is welcomed and made much of. We should therefore examine the objectives of, and objections to, nursery education very carefully. Is it true that it is harmful to separate children from their mothers before the age of two or three? Are they upset at going to nursery school or into day care? Should society attempt to

162

provide places for all children whose parents choose to avail themselves of them, or only step in to prevent dire hardship? On the positive side does nursery education give children a head start in primary education? Are there long-term effects on the children's educational progress or on the development of personality? Or is it the case that neither good nor bad long-term effects on the children can be demonstrated, and that advocacy of public services for young children should be on grounds of parental choice and well-being rather than for any supposed effects for good or ill on the children?

In this chapter and the next two we consider these questions, first, as they bear upon the extent of provision that is required, secondly, as they relate to objectives, organisation and achievements.

What the parents want

Elsewhere we have summarised changes taking place in the way of life of parents of young children which influence needs for services of various kinds. The concept of need is of course an elusive one since needs depend upon expectations as well as on circumstances defined in other ways. However, in estimating how much nursery provision was required, Plowden was greatly influenced by its assessments of parental wishes: it was estimated that half of the parents of three year old children and 90% of those of four year olds would wish their children to have nursery education. What is the situation today?

The data upon which the Plowden estimates of parental wishes were based were not very firm — and changes in family structure, parental expectations, and work habits over the last decade have already made them obsolete. Today we have better data from Britain, and we can examine trends in other countries similar to our own which provide a check on estimates of demand made in this country.

During the last two years, a number of surveys have been carried out in different parts of England: they give a generally consistent picture. The following table presents estimates which Peter Moss and Ian Plewis of the Thomas Coram Research Unit have made on the basis of interviews undertaken by staff of the Unit in three areas of London. The localities differed considerably in social class composition and housing; but the data from the surveys are so similar that the results can be pooled.

Percentage of children whose mothers want pre-school provision for them in three areas of London, 1974-5, by age of child.

Hours wanted per day	Age of child	0-1 N=90 children	1-2 N=73 children	2-3 N=97 children	3-4 N=98 children	4-5 N=94 children	All Ages N=452 children
None		83	56	27	10	9	36
1,2		0	1	8	7	4	5
3,4		1	9	23	36	27	20
5,6		0	8	8	24	36	15
7+		16	26	34	23	24	24
TOTAL		100	100	100	100	100	100
Per cent demanding services		17	44	73	90	91	64
Per cent attending services		6	21	43	72	80	46

This table shows several striking features. First, as shown in the last but one row of the table, 64 per cent of mothers of all children under five desire some form of nursery service. Though only 17 per cent of mothers of children under one year of age and 44 per cent of mothers of one year olds express a desire for such a service, the proportion rises to 73 per cent for two year olds and to over 90 per cent for three and four year olds. Secondly, the demand for part-time places (less than 4 hours) is for only a minority of children in all age groups. The highest demand for all ages is for provision lasting a school day or longer; 5 hours a day or more is wanted for 42% of two year olds and rises to 60% for four year olds. The slightly anomalous pattern for 7+ hours (all day as opposed to school-day care), where demand rises up to three years, then falls back, may be due to the acceptance of, and adjustment to, what is in reality available for the over-threes. In most cases this is full or part-time schooling, a maximum of 5-6 hours a

164

day, supplemented by other, informal methods of child care if needed. At present part-time education is being encouraged both by central and local government. However, as these figures — and the empty places in some part-time nursery schools — indicate, it is not something that most mothers find useful. Thirdly, a comparison of demand with attendance shows that unsatisifed demand is proportionately greater for children under three, which reflects the general dearth of part-time and full-time provision for younger children.

Despite the gap between demand and attendance, it should be noted that attendance figures for all age groups in the three areas surveyed are already relatively high: just under a half of two year olds and three-quarters of three and four year olds attended some sort of pre-school provision (including minders). These attendance rates are much higher than those in the country as a whole.

Two further points not shown in the table came out of the surveys. First, there was no marked social class gradient in the level of demand — middle-class mothers were as likely as working-class mothers to want pre-school provision, though working-class mothers tended to want longer hours. Secondly, among mothers of children of all ages who sought day-care and education outside the family for their children, there was a marked preference in favour of care in nurseries or playgroups rather than daily minding (even with a registered minder).

These estimates of demand are very much higher than those given in the Plowden Report or the targets set for day nursery expansion, but they are in line with trends elsewhere in the industrial world (see Chapter 6). Probably Plowden under-estimated demand. And probably demands have also changed. In the absence of adequate services, however, one cannot say how far these *expressed* demands reflect what the take-up of services would be if they were readily available on a non-selective and flexible basis.

Effects of separation upon children

As well as what parents might want, we also have to consider the dual effect on the children of separation from the mother and care by some other person outside the home. The contro-versy about whether mothers should work or not is in essence

165

a facet of this larger argument. It involves consideration of social class attitudes and behaviour, the nature of substitute care, the age at which a child should be permitted (or encouraged) to attend a nursery centre, and the length of time he can be allowed to stay without detriment to his development and wellbeing. On the latter two issues, Plowden was exceedingly cautious: not before the child was three, and in general not for more than half a day.

The psychological grounds on which recommendations such as these have been made have been stated many times, but perhaps nowhere more forcefully than by the Expert Committee on Mental Health of the World Health Organisation in its 1951 Report. The WHO Committee based its views very largely on the influential report on 'maternal deprivation' which had just been published by Bowlby (1951). This dealt very largely with residential care, but the conclusions were extended by others, including the WHO Expert Committee, to all forms of experience involving separation of the young child from his mother.

The most common reason for sending a young child under two or three to a day nursery, the Committee noted is:

> to free the mother to go out to work. In such a case the separation of mother and child is a daily occurrence, which some children cannot tolerate, being upset and crying for most of the day. The mother of such a child is likely to go to work with a feeling of guilt.
>
> The health worker should understand the significance of this daily separation and should be able to support both mother and child through a trying experience. If the child cannot adjust quickly to the situation separation should not be continued. There is an opposite danger. The health worker should recognise that a disturbed child who quickly settles down into a docile and spiritless form of behaviour may be suffering psychological damage even more serious than the child who remains aggressive and defiant.
>
> There is one other aspect of this problem upon which the committee feels it to be its duty to comment. At the present time the social and fiscal policy of many nations appears to be designed to press the mothers of pre-school children to

undertake productive work outside the home. The provision of creches and day nurseries is often one of the instruments of government policy in encouraging such a tendency. . . . The committee is convinced that in many instances such a decision . . . has been taken in complete ignorance of the price to be paid in permanent damage to the emotional development of a future generation. It should be the duty of national public health administrations to ensure that such a decision is taken only in full knowledge of all its implications.

The WHO Committee qualified its generalisations by reference to national considerations regarding the importance of industrial productivity. However they left no doubt about what they themselves thought: who in their right mind would advocate increased production if the price to be paid for it was 'permanent damage to the emotional development of a future generation'?

A great deal of research carried out during the last twenty-five years (and admirably summarised and discussed by Rutter, 1972) has led psychologists to reassess such generalisations about the supposed short-term and long-term effects of 'maternal deprivation'; it is clear today that the questions they raise are much more complex than the early formulations of the problems presupposed them to be. As Rutter puts it:

Children do not suffer from having several mother-figures so long as stable relationships and good care are provided by each. Indeed some studies have shown that children of working mothers may even be *less* likely to become delinquent than children whose mothers stay at home. In these circumstances it seemed that the mother going out to work was a reflection of a generally high standard of family responsibility and care. Two provisos need to be made with respect to these studies. First, there has been little investigation of the effects of mothers starting work while their children are still infants, although such data as are available do not suggest any ill-effects. Second, a situation in which mother-figures keep changing so that the child does not have the opportunity of forming a relationship with any of them may be harmful. Such unstable arrangements usually occur in association with poor-quality maternal care, so that it has not been possible to examine the effects of each independently.

Much the same can be said about the effects of day nurseries and creches (as particular forms of care often used when mothers go out to work). Assertions in official reports (WHO Expert Committee on Mental Health, 1951) concerning their permanent ill-effects are quite unjustified. Day care need not necessarily interfere with the normal mother-child attachment and the available evidence gives no reason to suppose that the use of day nurseries has any long-term psychological or physical ill-effects.

During the early 1950s it was insufficiently realised that the evidence assembled by Bowlby was drawn almost exclusively from institutional studies carried out in residential units which offered care that was psychologically of exceedingly poor quality, however well-intentioned. And it would seem that where the earlier studies went wrong was in equating a particular type of care outside the family (in this case the old-fashioned institution with its poor facilities, inadequate staffing, and high staff turnover, and its gross neglect of individual children's needs) with all forms of 'substitute' child care. The central issue is, however, the quality of care, not the place in which it is offered. Today the classical controversies among psychologists about the dangers of any form of maternal separation during the child's earliest years have given way to more detailed empirical studies of particular aspects of the environment which appear to influence particular aspects of the child's development.

The earlier controversies did however have one very important outcome: they caused those concerned with the planning of nursery services to consider much more carefully than ever they had in the past the kind of environment that would best meet the needs of young and immature children. It came to be recognised that the longer the time the young child spends away from his own home the more account has to be taken of his need for security and continuity in adult relationships. The problem of how to ensure these, arises in an extreme form in the case of children who go into residential care; but the needs of young children in all-day care for stability and continuity of relationships are also taxing ones.

We do, however, have a clear idea of the main steps that require to be taken in order to meet these needs. In a seminal publication on young children in *residential* nurseries during the second world war, Dorothy Burlingham and Anna Freud (1944) laid down two cardinal principles which provide the guidelines for current nursery practice. One related to the manner in which young children should be introduced into residential or nursery settings, the other to the way in which they should continue to be cared for in them. It is, the authors say,

> not so much the fact of separation to which the child reacts abnormally as the form in which the separation has taken place. The child experiences shock when he is suddenly and without preparation exposed to dangers with which he cannot cope emotionally . . . unsatisfied longing produces in him a state of tension which is felt as shock.
>
> If separation happens slowly, if the people who were meant to substitute for the mother were known to the child beforehand, the transition from one object to another would proceed gradually. If the mother reappeared several times during the period when the child has to be weaned from her, the pain of separation would be felt each successive time in smaller doses. By the time the affection of the child has let go of the mother the new substitute-object would be well known and ready to hand. There would be no empty period in which the feelings of the child are completely turned inwards and consequently there would be little loss of educational achievement. Regression happens when the child passes through the no-man's land of affection, i.e. during the time after the old object has been given up and before the new one has been found.

Freud and Burlingham were writing about residential settings, but what they say applies equally to day care: and in all good nursery settings today, whether part-time or full-time, day or residential, mothers do remain with their children while they settle in, and reappear from time to time so that the child can gradually accustom himself to her absence. How long this may take will depend on the child and on the nursery. Some children settle almost at once, others adjust only slowly. But very few indeed are unable to do so at all.

Likewise, whilst a child remains in a nursery setting, every effort is made to ensure that he receives continuity of care from a small number of familiar people. The number of adults 'handling' the child is kept to a minimum consistent with good child care, and the group — of adults and children — remains small and has as few changes as possible in order that the child may familiarise himself with his companions and develop relationships with them. The younger the child, the smaller the primary group with which he can identify. But all young children are more comfortable in small groups than in large ones, and most large day nurseries are divided into smaller groups in which children can feel a sense of belonging

In short, there is substantial evidence (well reviewed in Rutter, 1972) that to remove a young child abruptly to a strange residential institution is psychologically harmful; that long-stay care in an intellectually impoverished environment, whether day or residential, has a stultifying effect upon the development of intelligence; and that children who have frequent changes in adult care and who are not given the opportunity to form affective bonds with an adult who remains in their lives at least during their childhood are likely to develop differently from other children — and perhaps the marked differences from normal personality development which are found in a substantial proportion of institutional children could be described as more or less pathological. Equally, however, it can be said even of residential upbringing that the trauma of separation can be greatly eased if, as Freud and Burlingham point out, this takes place gradually; that residential upbringing in well-run nurseries can have a stimulating rather than a retarding effect on intellectual development (B. Tizard, et al 1972); that early intellectual privation can be remedied at least in large part if the child's subsequent intellectual diet is a nourishing one (Clarke and Clarke, 1974); and that children adopted from residential nurseries between the ages of two and four are able to develop normally, both

170

intellectually and emotionally (B. Tizard, 1975-6). That is, even *residential* care need not be traumatic, though it often is; and recovery from the effects of adverse circumstances in early childhood can occur, though it often does not. To a young child, residential care in a nursery in which staff are bound to change and in which he has few opportunities to receive the undivided attention of a parent figure is unsatisfactory. But there are worse things that can happen to him; and even residential care is likely to be better than the only alternative offering for a small number of children in the most adverse home circumstances.

Any effects found as a consequence of residential care occur in greatly attenuated form in children admitted to day care. Even infants under the age of twelve months can rapidly settle happily to having a nanny *and* a mother who take turns in looking after them, and this is true of older children also — as families who employ servants have always known. To require children to adjust both to a different adult and in a different environment is of course more difficult and needs more time and skill. But settling a child into a good nursery in which care is individual and attentive is not impossible — and for the child it need not be painful. If the child's developmental skills and needs for affection and individual care and attention are respected, and if placement is not hurried, it is likely to be successful in that the child will soon enjoy going to the centre and not be disturbed when he returns home. It seems not unlikely that more children are disturbed on entering primary school at age five than are upset by going to nursery school. If this is so, it would suggest that what is important in determining the child's adjustment to school is not simply his age, but the ability of the institution to meet the needs of the child at that particular level of development. And as we point out in Chapter 10, teachers in nursery schools are particularly sensitive to the emotional needs of young children.

As for long-term effects upon social and emotional development of good nursery education, or good day care, the evidence is fairly conclusive that they are minimal. Numerous reviews of nursery programmes carried out in the United States (e.g. Bronfenbrenner, 1975) have shown this, as have the studies carried out in this country (Plowden Report; Van der Eyken, 1974). The follow-up studies of traditional nursery education refute the dire predictions of those who claim that early separation from the parents has a crippling effect on a child's subsequent personality development. Equally they dash the hopes of those who believe that a year or two in the emotionally benign atmosphere of a good school will provide such a sound basis for subsequent character-formation that children who have had such experiences will be less prone to neuroses, less often delinquent, and better prepared for the vicissitudes of life in primary school. There is no really good evidence that these desirable outcomes occur, and it is entirely unreasonable to 'evaluate' nursery services by reference to such long-term 'criteria'. The immediate benefits of good nursery care, both to children and their parents, are manifest — and whether in any particular case a family chooses to avail itself of services that are offered can well be left to the good sense of the family and the community. We can be confident that if the happiness and wellbeing of parents and children are enhanced at the time, no covert ill effects are likely to follow later.

The problems of deciding what kind of nursery service we require, of measuring function and 'outcomes' in order to select a range of services which will best meet society's needs, are of a different order from those we have so far discussed. To these we now turn.

Given the manifest and politically recognised need for services for young children, the first task would seem to be to decide to what ends these services should aspire. However, education has always been unwilling to declare its aims — on the grounds that for education, as for life itself, a listing of 'objectives' is bound to be unsatisfactory. For all that, as organisational sociologists have pointed out, every social institution must in fact serve social functions, even if its goals are not explicitly formulated. So what are the objectives of nursery practice, and upon what bases are its foundations laid today?

Knowledge of the *conditions* required for the satisfactory development of young children is very considerable. Infant mortality statistics provide an indication of the medical advances that have been made during the present century: in 1900 one in every six or seven babies died during the first year of life; today one in sixty. The baby's need for physical care, for adequate and appropriate food, for regular sleep, for appropriate clothing, for activity, for sensori-motor stimulation, for a linguistically and cognitively rich environment, and for an interesting, secure and varying social environment — these matters are discussed in every book and article on parentcraft. There is, likewise, an extensive popular literature on the development of children from babyhood through the toddler age to the talkative independence and rapidly growing competence of the three and four year old child of 'pre-school age'.

Neuro-motor and psychological development is also well charted, 'milestones' of development having been adequately described, particularly by Gesell, whose neuro-developmental studies have most clearly stated (indeed over-stated) the innate programming of the sequences of growth as they manifest

173

themselves in the 'stages' of development during the first five years. In like manner developmental psychologists, influenced most notably by the work of Piaget, have described sequences or stages of sensori-motor understanding and cognitive development. But though developmental neurology and genetic psychology ostensibly provide the main theoretical bases for the subject of child development on which today's nursery education draws, how much these disciplines have contributed to actual nursery practice is questionable. For the principles of child care and nursery education were formulated long before men ever began to study developmental paediatrics and child psychology, and changes in nursery practice have come about less because of changes in the theories of child development, than because of changes in our thinking about the role of children in society, and from the lessons of experience gained in attempting to provide for their needs. Paediatrics, and child psychology, have been used to justify rather than to determine the nursery curriculum.

Child-centred nursery practice: learning through play

If neither developmental neurology nor cognitive child psychology has done more than provide a theoretical validation for nursery practice, two other influences have been of great importance, both in determining aims and in moulding the curriculum. The first was the writing of Froebel, the second the theory of psychoanalysis. It was Froebel in 1826 who first argued that nursery education should be *child centred,* and that since the young child demonstrated through his own activity that he learned and developed through play, the curriculum of the nursery school should be one which provided optimal opportunities for him to do so. According to Froebel, a satisfactory system of education and care for the young is based on the bio-social development of the child; the task of child care and education is to provide an environment that optimises growth and development, and enables the child to construct his world through play — which is 'the work of the child'.

The continuing influence of Froebel can be seen in all subsequent educational writings dealing with young children. The Plowden Report (Central Advisory Council on Education,

1967) for example, writes about the education of young children in terms that might well have been taken straight from Froebel's *The Education of Man,* written more than a century previously:

> At the heart of the educational process lies the child. . . . Play is the central activity in all nursery schools and in many infant schools. . . . We know that play is vital to children's learning and therefore vital in school . . . . Adults who criticise teachers for allowing children to play are unaware that play is the principal means of learning in early childhood. . . . The child is the agent in his own learning. . . . The strongest influence making for the free day has been the conviction of some teachers and other educationalists that it is through play that young children learn.

The manner in which current nursery practice uses play as its main medium of education has been well described by Gardner (1948). She was writing about nursery *schools* but what she says would apply equally to current practice in other forms of nursery service. The nursery school, according to Gardner, is based on the idea of providing not a substitute for but an extension of the home. It is therefore made as homelike as possible, not only in the type of building, which gives the child easy access to the garden and provides cheerful playrooms, but in the still more important matter of the relations between teachers and child. The nursery school teacher knows that she will often be called upon to act as a wise mother and is ready to give comfort and warm affection expressed in caresses at times of distress; but she respects the child's desire for independence when he feels happy and secure, and she encourages the whole of the domestic staff of the school to be interested in the children also.

The nursery school aims at providing conditions for development which the busy mother is unable to provide when she is absorbed in domestic duties. The intellectual development of young children, Miss Gardner says, is largely dependent on active experiments which would lead them into danger if undertaken in the normal home kitchen. So the school provides an environment which is planned to suit the needs of children, and in which experiment can be freely and safely permitted.

The pace of life in the nursery school is also suited to the capacities of young children, and the teacher is free from the mother's preoccupations with the daily round of work, so she can watch and encourage experiments and answer the torrent of questions with which the three year old tends to assail the adult. Relations between mother and child are strengthened by relieving the mother of the child's ceaseless questions and experiments during the busy middle hours of the day, and the child is guarded against the danger of his damping down curiosity and effort, in order to please his mother, during these very important and formative years.

Young children enjoy and benefit from the companionship of children of their own age. They are apt to become retarded in social development and to feel afraid of, or hostile towards, other children unless they meet them regularly in friendly play. The child in the nursery school experiences living in a community where turns must be taken, and other children's rights recognised, before he is plunged into school life at the age of five. He also becomes accustomed to friendly relations with adults. Because of all this experience, Miss Gardner says, nursery school children are noticeably more confident and co-operative on entering school than those who enter straight from home. (Others have found the evidence for this less convincing — see Thompson, 1975.)

Dorothy Gardner describes a typical day in a nursery school, and goes on to say that it may appear as if little attention is paid to actual learning —but the belief is that play is the finest of all education and can include the best beginning in all the 'subjects' of later study. Speech and language are not neglected, though it is no longer attempted to provide for them by special lessons but rather through informal talk with the children about their play and at meals and in the toilet room. Nor she adds, is it now believed that the child's intelligence is developed, or his knowledge increased, by the performance of graded exercises with particular apparatus. Instead, it is thought that the child learns best through occupations which he seeks for himself. Accordingly the teachers try, while watching these occupations, to give the child scope for full intellectual satisfaction, making their own contribution as they see his needs. He is encouraged to help the teachers and other children, but not so much by a set procedure of domestic occupations and systematic waiting at table as by using those occasions when needs for helpfulness arise of which the children are aware.

> We aim at good friendly feeling rather than set habits. So the younger and older children are encouraged to play together during part of the day because this is thought to be good for both. However it is realised that the little ones need quiet and leisure and close contact with a grownup for part of the time, while the older ones need opportunities for more boisterous play and for intellectual experiments which would be hampered by the constant presence of the little ones.

In her book with Joan Cass, Dorothy Gardner (Gardner and Cass, 1965) described changes in English infant and nursery schools during the forty years or so after the first world war, and the evolution of the doctrine of play. She divided the development into four periods. First, in infant schools but not nursery schools, was the period of class teaching. Oral lessons, usually short in duration, were interspersed with periods of physical activity or 'occupation', but even in these periods the whole class would be engaged in the same set of physical exercises or the same 'occupation'. This type of teaching was often carried out with great skill and warm humanity, but it was manifestly unsuccessful in the impossible task of securing uniformly good results from all members of the class.

Secondly, and largely under the influence of Montessori, it came to be realised that it was possible even in large classes to have the children busily and purposefully occupied while the teacher remined in the background helping children individually. This demanded of the teacher mastery of the art of organising and planning an environment suited to children, and a deep understanding of the needs of children as individuals.

The third stage was brought about by the impact of the 'project method' as emphasised by Dewey. Progressive infant teachers were quick to appreciate the value of the project method, which harnessed to the core of education the tremendous drive and energy of the children, once they were deeply concerned about finding out certain things and gaining certain skills for ends which they themselves appreciated. However, teachers became aware that they, the adults, had still to play a too-dominant role in the class if they were to keep all children working with the same end in view. It came to be realised that the real interests of different children were either different from the beginning, or became so, well before the project which the teacher had planned had been completed. It was in short difficult to sustain all the children's interest in a project which owed its inspiration to the teacher. There were other problems too; and the project method, which never had a very fundamental influence on nursery schools, was finally largely abandoned in the infant school also.

A variant of the project method which *was* tried in some nursery schools involved basing each week's programme on a 'centre of interest'. These were not generally successful, and teachers soon found that what the children really wanted to do was generally equally rich in educational possibility if fostered and encouraged intelligently. The nursery and infant school therefore moved on to a fourth stage, one which allowed the older as well as the young infant school children, as well as children of nursery age, a great variety of choice. Susan Isaacs' work at the Malting House School in Cambridge, which illustrated very clearly how often the highest peaks of the child's thought and learning were found in the situation of spontaneous purposeful play, was particularly influential in bringing about this change.

Gardner's summary of the central part taken by play in nursery education still meets with almost universal acceptance among nursery teachers. A recent and authoritative statement to this effect has been given by Marianne Parry and Hilda Archer (1974) in the Report of their survey of 'good practice' in pre-school education carried out under the sponsorship of the Schools Council. It is, they say,

178

the joy and pleasure of play which sets the stage for learning
and through play the child finds opportunities to explore
materials, to create, to construct, to destroy and discover. . . .
The child learns how to mix with other children by sharing
experiences with them, discovering how friendships occur,
witnessing how other children behave, particularly when
their wishes are opposed to his.

It is through play that he integrates and patterns the scattered
information he receives from the environment, in his own time,
and at his own pace. In his play the child learns skills which
are necessary in the complex world in which he lives; his play
becomes a direct path to his cognitive growth.

The psycho-analytical justification of play

Parry and Archer stress the value of play in providing a medium
through which social and cognitive skills are learned and prac-
tised. But many writers go further than this and see the
primary virtues of play as symbolic and therapeutic, enabling
the child to act out his fears and fantasies. This view, which
seems incapable of rigorous testing though it is easy to get
anecdotal evidence in support of it, is due largely to the
influence of psycho-analytic theory. Thus Isaacs (1930)
following Melanie Klein, regarded much of the child's earliest
interest in physical objects as 'derivative', drawing its impetus
from early infantile wishes and fears in relation to its parents.

> The *first* value which the physical world has for the child
> is as a canvas upon which to project his personal wishes
> and anxieties, and his first form of interest in it is one of
> dramatic representation . . . . Engines and motors and fire
> and lights and water and mud and animals have a pro-
> foundly symbolic meaning, rooted in infantile phantasy. . . .
> In their free dramatic play, children work out their inner
> conflicts in an external field thus lessening the pressure of
> the conflict, and diminishing guilt and anxiety.

From this, says Isaacs, it follows that it would be a serious
mistake to try to make children follow prescribed courses of
instruction, or master skills which are selected by adults.

179

'They must be given a large measure of freedom to imagine or to think as the occasion arises. If we tried to *teach* them these things formally, or to exert pressure on them in these directions, we should simply waste our time, and might even do positive harm.'

Elsewhere Isaacs (1932) states her view even more explicitly: 'Walking and running, jumping and climbing, throwing and balancing, threading beads and drawing — each is tried and attained in its turn. We don't have to teach children to do these things. They do them, with passion and delight, if we leave them room and opportunity.' Our role is only to observe the children so that 'we can give them things to do and to play with, which will feed their skills and power.'

Isaacs' views about play and education, and those of the psycho-analytic school generally, have had a profound influence on nursery practice. Taken literally, as they often are, they completely rule out *instruction* in the nursery school; the teacher guides but does not teach, provides a setting but scarcely a model, enables but rarely prescribes. The initiative rests with the child — and if the child fails to grasp the opportunities that are made available to him in the nursery setting, an easy interpretation of his behaviour in terms of 'readiness', or stages, or unconscious conflicts, or prepotent fantasies, can at once be offered. He is said not to be 'ready' to do so, not at that stage of development, or too caught up in unconscious conflicts which require to be worked through, and so on.

From this it readily follows that the aims of nursery education became personal and subjective: to further development; to enable the child to fulfil his potential; to optimise growth; to come to terms with reality; to resolve internal conflicts. Whereas in the nursery centre established by Robert Owen, or in the day nursery school set up by Margaret McMillan in Deptford a century later, children engaged in many group activities and were taught a good deal in an informal way, this is much less true of nursery education today. It is not surprising therefore that assessments of whether young children benefit from nursery experience (if by benefit is meant improving their language skills, or even their social adjustment as assessed by their behaviour in other situations) are little favoured.

Contemporary child psychology is increasingly critical of this way of looking at the functions of play; and indeed even the view that children learn mainly through play is one which has been challenged in recent yrears, particularly by American child psychologists. British nursery school practice is however still greatly influenced by these views, though perhaps less strongly than was the case a few years ago.

The evaluation of nursery schooling

Since the aims of early childhood education and care are usually expressed in such global terms as being 'to ensure that each child develops to his full capacity' it follows, as Parry and Archer point out, that no clearly defined results are to be expected. Nor, they add, is it always possible to make valid assessments of the nursery teacher's work: a too-scientific structured approach, they say, can actually interfere with the atmosphere in which the young child learns best. To critics who have protested that these aims are all much too vague and general, and that one function of nursery education should be to ensure that at least the *disadvantaged* child should learn in the nursery school the skills which will put him on an equal footing with his peers when he starts primary school at five, one answer that has been given is that we should change the primary schools, not attempt to force children into a new and alien culture.

We do have large numbers of children who start life at a disadvantage, for many and varied reasons, compared with other children, and all the evidence we have shows that these children remain at a disadvantage throughout their school. But, because we do not have grade requirements, we can adapt the school to suit the child, rather than the other way round. Since the thirties this has been the choice increasingly favoured by teachers in this country, first in nursery schools, later in infant and junior schools. We have a long way to go in this respect. Many teachers are hesitant about how far to go to meet the child, how far in whole-heartedly accepting what he brings with him in terms of language, culture, interests, concerns. Would minority children remain at a disadvantage in education if, right from the start, we fully accepted and respected them and what they bring into the school situation? We have much to learn in this basic issue of making education meaningful and worthwhile to children of parents from varied social and cultural backgrounds. Early childhood education can play a vital part here by its re-thinking and re-shaping, and, possibly most important of all, by fully involving parents from the beginning, not only in the day-to-day work of the school as welcome visitors, observers, helpers, but in our planning of the work (L. Steiner, 1973).

This view of early education — indeed of all education — has the great merit of respecting the child, of not denying or belittling the values of his family and his culture. Like all good education it would have us start with the child as he is, not with how the teacher would wish him to be. It does not think it necessary to destroy the child in order to recreate him. But having said that, it falters, slips into vagueness, takes refuge in beliefs which are at best unproven and probably false. It leaves to the child the task of determining educational aims, not the teachers or society, or even the parents. And if the child doesn't learn? If the parents have no 'ambition' for their children? If their ambitions are unrealistic or harmful — what then?

Progressive thinkers in the nineteenth century and much of the twentieth believed that education was a great leveller in the sense that it offered the children of each generation the chance to make up for the inequalities into which they were born. A measured statement of this view was put by Robbins (1963), and what his Report says about students in higher education could be applied with equal force to young children:

Finally there is a function that is more difficult to describe concisely, but that is none the less fundamental: the transmission of a common culture and common standards of citizenship. By this we do not mean the forcing of all individuality into a common mould: that would be the negation of higher education as we conceive it. But we believe that it is a proper function of higher education, as of education in schools, to provide in partnership with the family that background of culture and social habit upon which a healthy society depends. This function, important at all times, is perhaps especially important in an age that has set for itself the ideal of equality of opportunity. It is not merely by providing places for students from all classes that this ideal will be achieved, but also by providing, in the atmosphere of the institutions in which the students live and work, influences that in some measure compensate for any inequalities of home background. These influences are not limited to the student population. Universities and colleges have an important role to play in the general cultural life of the communities in which they are situated.

The danger in the 'new' progressive thinking is that in practice it may deny the children access to these skills and values, without offering anything in their place except an easier adjustment to the subculture. Unfortunately the belief that children 'know best' what is good for them, that they will 'naturally' learn intellectual and social skills at their own pace and in their own time, just as they learn to walk and to feed themselves, expresses only a very partial truth; it is also an expression of a false and sentimental notion about man and about society — one which was first enunciated by Rousseau and which is no more valid today than it was two hundred years ago.

To us it seems that something more is to be desired of nursery education. Its primary functions as we see them are to provide children with a safe, stimulating and enjoyable environment, and the companionship of other young children, under the guidance of competent and congenial adults, outside the home — and if nursery centres do no more than this they will be well worth the money society spends on them. But surely they should also aspire to compensate in some measure for the inequalities in home background by ensuring that all children who attend at least learn age-appropriate skills. It is not the job of the nursery to solve the problems of the primary school; it *is* one job of the nursery to see that its graduates are not more disadvantaged than they need be.

The word 'disadvantage' is widely used in the nursery literature. Its implications we discuss in the next chapter.

183

In this chapter we question the utility of the concept of disadvantage for education and child care, and then we consider whether or not it is possible, through nursery services, to raise the behavioural competencies of poorly functioning children. This leads us on to a broader consideration of the role of such services in a programme of ecological intervention designed to reduce social injustice and inequality. We also return to what is a major theme of this whole book, namely the view that nursery goals should be modest and immediate ones concerned above all with the happiness, wellbeing and development of young children and their families at the time, rather than with hoped-for long-term benefits. We believe that those who seek to evaluate nursery services by reference to the children's later success in primary school, rather than their wellbeing at the time, are inevitably led to minimise the importance of early childhood; it comes to be seen not as itself an exquisite part of life, with its own purposes and values, but as a mere preparation for supposedly more important things to come. This we simply do not accept. Nor do we regard the wellbeing or unhappiness of *parents* of young children as being of little account, even if it can be argued that things may well improve for them once their children are all at school, or have left home, or once they themselves have retired. For parents, as for children, the deep satisfactions of life are those they actually experience.

There is a further reason for asserting the primacy of concurrent satisfactions and short-term goals for our nursery services. It is that the arguments that a stimulating and satisfying environment early in life will in itself in some way see a child through to adolescence irrespective of what happens to him in the meantime are unconvincing, and are not supported by evidence. We would not, for example, expect that good infant feeding would in itself protect a child from starving if he were ill-fed later, nor for that matter do we expect university graduates to be able to pass their final examinations again three years after graduation. Why do we think differently about young children? There is of course a case to be made for assessing long-term outcomes; and well-substantiated findings would clearly be of interest in themselves, and relevant to the planning of the nursery curriculum. But we suspect that the current fashion for evaluation based almost exclusively on IQ changes and later educational attainments continues not because anyone believes that nothing else is important, but simply because IQ and educational measures exist, while there are no handy, ready-made and easily administered measures of other outcomes.

What little we know of the long-term consequences of early patterns of care challenges by implication the views both of the psycho-analysts and of cognitive theorists such as Bloom (1964) and Hunt (1961) that patterns of reaction laid down in early childhood are later irreversible: the evidence regarding long-term effects of deprivation, or lack of experience in early childhood, cannot be construed in such simple terms. It should also be noted that what appears to be a telling argument in support of early childhood intervention, namely that unless we start in infancy the children will suffer irretrievable damage, is likely to turn out to be a very bad one in practice as well as in theory. If, for example, it is found that the supposed long-term effects — beneficial if intervention takes place, adverse if it does not — do not in fact occur, the value of the intervention itself may be discounted. This is what is happening following the long-term evaluation of head start.

The concept of disadvantage

The word disadvantage, like the word love, evokes powerful vibrations. But in our view it is a term with so many and such varied meanings that it is of little use either in the planning of services for priority groups, or for the determination of the educational and child-care curriculum for children with special needs.

At one level, through a misunderstanding and misapplication

185

of the theories of Basil Bernstein, the term disadvantaged has been applied uncritically to virtually the whole of the working class — whose children make up 70 per cent of the child population (Plowden Report). If to these are added the children of single-parent families, of sick, neurotic or unhappy mothers or fathers, or those in difficulties of other sorts, it comes to embrace nearly everyone. If on the other hand, we select, as Wedge and Prosser (1973) did, four social indicators which in current conditions make it exceedingly difficult for most families to cope adequately, the proportion of disadvantaged children falls nationally to 6 per cent, though using the same criteria 10 per cent of all Scottish children are disadvantaged, and 16 per cent in Glasgow. (The criteria were: children who lived in one-parent families, or in families with five or more children, who in addition were poorly housed and had a low income.)

The criteria used by Wedge and Prosser are somewhat arbitrary, as they themselves recognise: why not four or six rather than five children, how poor is poor? And why just these criteria? Others have, for example, used somewhat different criteria, which will single out a somewhat different group of disadvantaged children: thus Harriett Wilson and G.W. Herbert (1975) have employed five indicators of social deprivation — father's degree of skill, family size, adequacy of clothing worn to school, truancy and parental contact with the school — to score children on an index of social deprivation. They show that even in an area of poverty and poor housing, in a run-down inner city borough, the 30 per cent of children with severe social handicaps were developmentally and educationally well below the 30 per cent of moderately handicapped children who in turn fell below the 40 per cent of those whose social disadvantages were least severe. The most and least severely handicapped differed in mean IQ by nearly 20 points, and the educational standards of the most disadvantaged were even more retarded than would have been predicted on the basis of IQ.

Others again have used the term disadvantaged to apply to children of parents born on the Indian subcontinent or in the West Indies — the descendants (mostly born in the UK) of former citizens of the New Commonwealth. These are the non-indigenous citizens of Britain, whom our laws endeavour to sort out on the basis of 'patriality' (the British equivalent of the Nuremberg race laws) or less ambiguously, colour.

In the country as a whole children of New Commonwealth parents constitute only 3.3 per cent of the total school population (on the basis of the DES definition — which takes into account the child's place of birth and length of residence in this country). Using a wider definition the proportion is 4.5 per cent (Community Relations Commission 1974). The distribution is, however, very uneven, more than half of the children being in London, and high proportions being in the West Midlands and South Lancashire. The CRC reports that two local authorities have more than 25 per cent of their pupil rolls defined as immigrant according to DES criteria, five between 20-25 per cent and a further six 15-20 per cent. Nearly 1,000 of 33,000 schools have over one-quarter immigrant pupils, and in some authorities one or two schools carry disproportionately high numbers whereas other schools have few.

The CRC argues that though in important respects many settlers from the New Commonwealth who live in depressed areas with whites share the characteristics of other socially and economically disadvantaged groups in society, and though not all recent settlers suffer disadvantages from their minority group status, nonetheless coloured or black children do have special problems of language and culture which contribute to their poor performance in school. And because they are visibly different they are also often subject to discrimination and hostility. The CRC therefore recommends that the existing educational system, its schools, staffing, curriculum and methods, must be modified to meet the needs of pupils from minority backgrounds — and they make detailed recommendations to deal with the problems of these disadvantaged groups. In arguing the case for special treatment for black children, the CRC makes a sharp distinction between their needs and those of other disadvantaged children. The Department of Education, however, in the White Paper *Educational Disadvantage and the Educational Needs of Immigrants*, hope to persuade LEAs to cope with these as part of a wider strategy of intervention designed to offset the educational disadvantage of a much larger and ill-defined group of children whatever their ethnic or social origin.

To equate disadvantage with skin colour, or immigrant status, has a certain validity in contemporary Britain. There is no doubt that many children of West Indian, Pakistani and Indian parents, like Chinese, Greek, Italian, Spanish, Portuguese and Turkish children, find it difficult to settle on an equal basis in British schools alongside children whose parents were themselves brought up in this country and who are culturally and linguistically assimilated. But the problems of children of West Indian parents, for example, are very different from those whose parents are from India; and though many families from 'minority cultures' are to be found among those singled out as disadvantaged by Wedge and Prosser, or by Harriett Wilson, or the DES, the groups selected according to the various criteria are by no means the same. Nor are they homogeneous.

Yet another way of singling out disadvantaged children is that employed by many social services departments in assigning priority for placement in day nurseries. These include (Ministry of Health circular 37/68) children whose mothers are sick or unable to look after them properly because they are incapable of doing so, or who are in danger of breakdown, and children whose home conditions are grossly overcrowded or whose health and welfare are seriously affected by a lack of opportunity for playing with others. As we have mentioned no estimate has been made of the numbers affected in these and other ways which are singled out for priority consideration. A target for day nursery places for children under five of 8 per 1,000 was given in a subsequent circular (35/72) but this is manifestly too low.

If, to select yet another disadvantaged group, we confine ourselves to children who themselves have chronic mental or physical handicaps of moderate or severe degree which are a cause of educational concern, as was done by Rutter and his colleagues in their epidemiological studies on the Isle of Wight (1970) and in London (1974), a still different selection of children will result: yet as these studies show, many children defined by these criteria as handicapped, are also educationally and socially disadvantaged in other ways, even though their parents may not be poor, or in unskilled occupations, or living in slums — or black.

The children in all of these groups, whether defined by the region in which they live, by area of residence in a city, or characteristics of housing, by parental occupation, country of origin, or mental or physical health, by family size or composition, by skin colour, or by the child's mental or physical handicap or educational or behavioural competencies, contain high proportions of children selected as disadvantaged according to other criteria. But they are not necessarily the same children, and their numbers differ greatly — as do their needs. As Rutter and Madge (1976) have pointed out in their masterly survey of 'cycles of disadvantage', the complexities of definition are very great; and these are compounded when one tries to assign causal significance to various factors associated with poor performance. When in addition we attempt to account for inter-generational consistencies, the facts themselves are in most cases not available, and the causal sequences are at best obscure.

It seems clear to us that the needs of disadvantaged children cannot be met by providing special services for children in 'priority' categories, however expedient it may be to do so to cope with the immediate problem. The difficulties of defining categories of priority and of finding and selecting children within these categories are insurmountable and such a system results in an inadequate service. Moreover, experience in other fields of social policy strongly suggests that selective services will in time come to have low standards: a service for the poor ends up as a poor service, whatever the hopes for it might have been. In any event, as we have argued throughout this book, the need for pre-school services is now a general one, and cannot be met by a system which chooses some children and denies others.

Strategies of intervention

In studies of day care and early child education undertaken with 'disadvantaged' children, very little attempt indeed has been made to analyse the characteristics of the cultural environment which are believed to be psychologically disadvantaging: nor have intervention strategies as a rule started with an

189

analysis of the children's various capacities and needs, and attempted to plan and carry through an interventionist curriculum designed specifically to remedy their alleged shortcomings. Instead, a different strategy has been employed. Urban slums or poor rural districts have been chosen as the target areas, and children in them selected on the basis of sex and age, parental social class, and in the United States where most of the work has been done, skin colour. Sometimes family composition and family size, and children's IQ (and more rarely, mothers' IQ) are also used as criteria, and sometimes only volunteer samples are studied. The progress of children in 'experimental' programmes is compared with that of children in 'control' nursery settings, or children who get no pre-school services at all.

A well-controlled British study may be cited to illustrate the strategy commonly adopted, and the results commonly obtained. It was carried out by H.L. Williams (to be published) and the following summary was made by B. Tizard (1975a) in her review of current British research in early child education.

Williams and his colleagues in the National Foundation for Educational Research carried out a study primarily to evaluate the effects of a nursery programme designed to reduce school failure in the primary school. The rationale was that school failure amongst disadvantaged children is related to their failure to acquire in their early years the basic repertoire of verbal, perceptual and conceptual skills and attitudes which are needed as a foundation for school success. It was hoped that the programme would present the children in a condensed form with the kind of experiences they were presumed to have missed at home. Stress was laid on both language and perceptual training.

A full year was spent in discussions with the teachers concerned, preparing and modifying the programme with their help. A modified version of the Peabody Language Development Kit (PLDK) was used, together with games for perceptual training. Small groups of children were taught with the PLDK for twenty minutes daily, and the nursery staff tried to reinforce the skills taught in these sessions at appropriate informal opportunities during the rest of the school day.

Perceptual training with the children took the form of graded series of games, which were conducted by nursery assistants under the supervision of the trained teachers. The experimental group was composed of 110 children; some had only one term of the programme before moving to primary schools, others had up to six terms. All the children, together with a control group of 81 children in another nursery school, were given an extensive battery of tests before starting on the programme and as they left for primary school. At the end of their first term in primary school the Boehm Test of Basic Concepts and a measure of adjustment to school were administered. At the end of their sixth term assessments of attainments in reading and number were obtained.

The full report on this study is not yet available , but some important findings have already emerged. The children in the programme made significant gains, compared to the control children who attended a traditional nursery school, on the Illinois Test for Psycho-linguistic Abilities (ITPA) language battery, and some of the perceptual tests. However, with the exception of the Verbal Expression sub-test of the ITPA, which is essentially a test of verbal fluency, the children who had spent only two terms in the programme made gains as large as those who had spent four or more terms. The social class gap in test scores was not closed, because children in all social classes made gains of a similar size. *But when tested at the age of seven there was no significant difference between the school attainments of the control children and those who had taken part in the programme. Moreover, teachers' ratings during the second half of the first term at primary school showed no difference in personal, emotional or social adjustment, between children who had attended either type of nursery school and children without any nursery school experience.*

The findings produced in this study are in full accord with those obtained in many American projects. Taking the evidence as a whole — and it is remarkably consistent — we can summarise the results to date as follows (J. Tizard, 1974):

First of all, ordinary nursery school experience does not in general result in increases in IQ or even in better educational

191

progress in primary school. Children may settle into school more easily, but the effects 'wash out' rather rapidly.

Secondly, special programmes for disadvantaged children do result in IQ rises of 5 to 15 points and sometimes even more. In general middle-class children show much more modest rises in IQ as a result of pre-school experiences, especially of the structured sort, though the evidence is not strong here.

However, children who have not had pre-school experience tend to show rises of between 5 and perhaps 8 points when they first enter school; that is, when they are exposed to formal education they too show modest IQ increments, especially if they come from disadvantaged homes.

Thirdly, the age and the duration of the intervention has not been shown to be crucial. That is, children who start in special programmes at the age of three tend to do no better than those who start at the age of four. This is a paradoxical finding, but it does seem to be borne out by the literature. Moreover, Bernstein's work [see Gahagan and Gahagan, 1970] with children in infant school. . . . also shows that you can get IQ changes following quite modest special programmes at ages five or six.

Fourthly, not much is known of what the Americans are now calling follow-through, though the first reports in the United States are beginning to come out. It does seem reasonably well established that the effects of special programmes tend to fade as children get older unless they are persisted in, and for this reason educators are now emphasising the importance of continuing special programmes for disadvantaged children through the years of primary schooling.

Another puzzling finding is that none of the special programmes, although they are ostensibly all very different, seem to show unequivocal advantages: it doesn't seem to matter which programme is pursued [possibly because in practice they mostly amount to much the same thing].

The sixth finding from the American literature relates to what Susan Gray has called diffusion effects. There is . . . evidence of two types of diffusion effect: one, that if you have a group of children in a neighbourhood who are given

192

special education, the effect tends to diffuse to other children in the neighbourhood; mothers talk about it and the other children get taught by their mothers to do the same kinds of things as the children in the programme are taught to do. This is a very important finding for educators. Something which is possibly even more significant in terms of its effects is that there are what Susan Gray calls vertical diffusion effects — mothers who have one child in a pre-school programme themselves learn something about child development and child management which they put into practice with subsequent children, who tend in consequence to be brighter and better able to cope than the older sibs.

There is also some evidence that whether or not pre-school programmes assist children when they start in primary schools is related to the similarity between what goes on in the pre-school setting and what happens once children enter compulsory school programmes. Some studies have shown that children do quite well during their first year if they have had pre-school experience; then the nature of the school regimen changes and their previous experience no longer equips them to deal with the new environment they meet at the age of, say, seven. Consequently they cannot cope with it.

How much is really feasible?   The Milwaukee Project

The modest short-term gains achieved in most experimental pre-school projects leave unanswered the question whether differently organised programmes, perhaps beginning earlier in the children's lives, perhaps continuing over a longer period of time, perhaps more systematically controlled and implemented, might not have greater and perhaps more long-lasting effects. If it is true, for example, that the majority of children growing up in the intellectually stimulating environment of middle-class homes achieve more than the majority of children growing up in lower-working-class homes partly (or wholly) because of the differences in their daily environment, then it might follow that 'disadvantaged' children who spent most of their waking lives in a really stimulating nursery might come to resemble their more fortunate peers who enjoyed such advantages in their own homes. It is this belief

193

that has motivated most of those who have attempted to devise 'compensatory' programmes — though, as we have seen, the programmes have, on the whole, offered too little to be really effective.

We do, nonetheless, have evidence, from clinical reports and from adoption and other studies, that environmental circumstances can and do exert profound effects upon the developmental competencies of children — and no one would dispute that this is so. But it is impossible, in the absence of strict experiment, with random allocation of cases to treatments, to know how far observed differences can be attributed to differences in their genetic make-up, and how far they are due to the modifying effects of environment. It has, for example, long been a common practice among adoption agencies to attempt to 'match' children and adoptive parents, children of professional parents being offered to adoptive parents in professional occupations, while those who are of working-class origin are offered to working-class adoptive parents. So it can be argued, because placement is not random, that differences in the children's later attainments may be due primarily to genetical factors in the children, rather than to differences in the adoptive homes the children are sent to. Similar objections can be raised over the interpretation of studies based on children growing up in foster homes and residential children's homes.

Criticisms of this sort are sometimes rather forced, and a number of studies have gone a long way to counter them. But, in the absence of experiment, with proper controls and random allocation to treatments, a purely genetical explanation of observed differences between groups growing up in different environments cannot be decisively rejected.

Of studies which satisfy the rigorous demands of an adequate experimental design, one is of such importance that it deserves a full summary. This is the Milwaukee Project, a study now being completed by Heber and Garber of the University of Wisconsin, who have during the last nine years been following the progress of two groups of children from very adverse backgrounds, one of which was subjected to a carefully constructed educational and day-care regimen while their matched controls were not. In this case the striking differences

194

in the performance of the two groups of children can almost certainly be attributed to the differences in their environment — though we cannot say what aspects of the environment were chiefly responsible, nor do we know what would happen to other children, of different genetical and social background, if they were given the same programme. The results to date, however, do suggest what short-term effects may be achieved from early, carefully structured and intensive intervention.

Because a full report of the Milwaukee Project is not easily available, and because of its intrinsic interest, the following summary presents its main features.

The Milwaukee Project, a longitudinal study which began in 1966, was designed to determine whether cultural, familial or socio-cultural mental retardation could be prevented through a programme of family intervention beginning in early infancy. Forty babies born to black mothers living in a slum area of Milwaukee, Wisconsin, all of whom had IQs below 75, were divided into two groups of 20. The experimental group was given a programme starting during the first few months of the child's life; the control group was assessed regularly but given no educational or other assistance. The experimental programme had two components: (1) an infant, early childhood stimulation programme; (2) a maternal rehabilitation programme. Though a full account of this study has not yet been made available a summary has been given by Heber and Garber (1975):

> For the newborn infant, the program's objective was to provide intensive language and sensory-motor stimulation, and thereby facilitate the development of cognitive skills. Each day, beginning as soon after birth as was feasible — usually between three and six months of age — the child was picked up at home and brought to the Infant Education Center for the entire day.
>
> The general educational program is best characterised as having a cognitive-language orientation implemented through a structured environment. Individualized prescriptive teaching techniques were utilised in the daily program (7 hours per day, 5 days per week). There was a high

teacher-to-child ratio, which gave flexibility to the program and allowed for teacher feedback on the effectiveness of methods as well as individualization of instruction.

The program for the Experimental mother was designed to prepare her for employment and increase her awareness of her environment. This program included vocational training and classes in homemaking and fundamental academic skills.

The Control children, drawn from the same group of families as the Experimentals, were seen only for testing, which was done on a prescribed schedule for both the Experimental and Control groups of children. The testing schedule consisted of a comprehensive array of standardised and non-standardised measures of behavioral development, and was set from infancy to age seven where independent behaviour evaluations are scheduled as the project's terminal point.

Our schedule of measurement included: (1) development schedules of infant adaptive behavior; (2) experimental learning tasks; (3) measures of language development; (4) measures of social development; and (5) standardised tests of general intellectual functioning.

In an earlier report Heber, Garber et al (1972) discuss in some detail the characteristics of the educational programme. They comment on its general features as follows:

> Although we discuss the curriculum in terms of separated areas and related activities, we designed the educational program so that the children were exposed to the widest range of experiences . . . . We have attempted to create a curriculum that combines aspects of many theories while at the same time remains flexible enough to be individualised for each child and for our group of children as a whole.
>
> Within the educational program, the general cognitive-language and social goals were similar for each child, yet no two children have been exposed to the same program. Since children learn at different rates (depending on many factors, among them activity, mood, time of day), and differ in

their style of learning, we attempted to maximize the effects of the educational experiences for each child. In practical terms, this meant that while all children experienced learning activities that were presented in small steps with opportunities for positive, supportive feedback, the breakdown of task components, the length of tasks, types of material used, size of group and methods of presentation varied from child to child and group to group . . . .

Subject areas were delineated for the purpose of organisation of the daily program. However, this should not imply that each content area was a discrete unit. All of the areas are closely inter-related, encompassing not only similar concepts but also similar processes. In infancy, emphasis was placed on cognitive-language, social-emotional and perceptual-motor development. In the pre-school years, the emphasis was on the breakdown of the cognitive-language area into three overlapping units, (reading, language, maths [problem-solving]) with perceptual-motor functioning and social-emotional growth underlying all areas of the curriculum.

The effect of this educational programme upon the children's development was remarkable. It was shown not only in the development of their tested intelligence, and in their language and other cognitive abilities, but in their social behaviour and their response to schooling.

The striking contrast with the control group can be seen most clearly from Heber and Garber's IQ data, reproduced in Figure 11.

Heber and Garber explain their findings by pointing to differences in the learning environment of the two groups of children.

The natural desire to pursue and discover and learn about one's world that is within each of us can be dampened or shut down by negative learning experiences. In all too many cases, a child's failure to learn may well be due to the restricted learning environment created for him in early life by a mother who is incapable of providing otherwise.

Figure 11: Mean IQ performance with increasing age

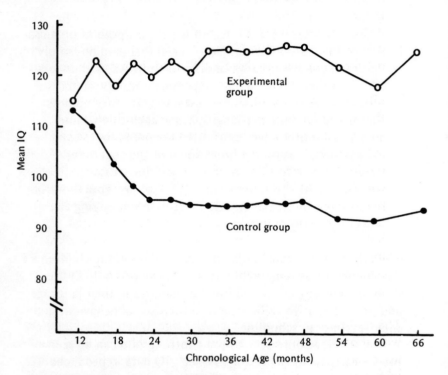

Redrawn from Heber, Garber *et al* (1972)

As a result, children who have such developmental histories develop a behavior system which is antagonistic to the learning they must do for successful school performance.

Learning need not be forced if there is excitement; experiences must not be restricted, rather opportunities for learning must be varied; solutions must have alternatives, and discovery must be shared in. The environment for a pre-school age child must be at once so rich, so varied, so intriguing, and so organized that a child has before him considerable opportunity to learn and make use of his own natural tendencies to discover. But this may not be possible where the mother is mentally retarded and creates a very different environment. It appears from our effort to date that the mitigation of the environmental influences for which cultural-familial retardation is a consequence can be accomplished if help is given to that large population of mothers who are unaware of the critical nature of early childhood and also unaware of their own needs during pregnancy. In large part, it is these mothers who consequently contribute to the growing number of children born at high risk for mental retardation, Therefore, existing early stimulation programs notwithstanding, there remains considerable need for comprehensive programs of prevention.

The results of this particular programme, taken in conjunction with those of many other experimental and longitudinal studies, leave very little doubt that a learning and social environment which is varied, stimulating and attractive to children can have a very marked effect indeed upon their functioning at the time. However, if substantial changes are to occur, the learning environment cannot be left largely to the child's initiative. Instead a rounded programme is required — one which will be interesting and satisfying to the child as well as cognitively appropriate, socially rich, adequate in its coverage — and fun to take part in. In British nurseries the very idea of programmes, or structure, is frowned upon by the teachers and professionals who staff them. Whether parents if given a choice would agree with the professionals is less certain.

What a programme means

To us it seems that the issue of programme and structure is wrongly posed today in the nursery literature. The choice is no longer between, on the one hand, a child-centred curriculum in which children create their own environment, and learn through active and sponaneous play, and on the other hand serried ranks of children sitting in tiered galleries performing meaningless tasks and chanting tables in unison. It is a gross misrepresentation of the best of today's structured programmes to portray them as consisting of boring tasks that the children are inveigled into doing by means of extrinisic reinforcements. The fact is, as Heber and Garber and others have pointed out, the children love them. Likewise it is sheer confusion of thought to maintain both that the nursery environment is the product of a great deal of careful planning based on observation and experience (as it undoubtedly is) and at the same time argue that it is the 'natural' environment for the child. It is certainly one which young children enjoy and use in their activities and play. But both the material environment and the social reinforcements of ways of using it are controlled in large measure by the adults — properly and necessarily so. Hence the child-centred nursery, no less than the most formal classroom, has its own curriculum. Where it may differ most from a curriculum of the type described by Heber and Garber may be in the extent to which there are any adult-child contacts at all.

The stimulating effect upon staff behaviour of working to a programme or plan of instruction has been demonstrated in the somewhat different context of American pre-school services, by Miller and Dyer (1970), who made a systematic point-by-point comparison of four types of programmes.

The traditional approach, they say, is

> largely distinguished from the rest on the basis of things that are not done. Video-tape monitoring of teacher behavior provides striking support for the ideological distinction. Teachers in the traditional program are not so much distinguished by differences in the relative frequency of different kinds of teaching (as are teachers in the other three programs) as by the generally low frequency of

teaching acts of any kind. The mean frequency of teaching acts of any kind among the traditional teachers is less than half that of teachers in the Bereiter-Engelmann classes (Miller and Dyer, 1970, cited by Bereiter, 1972).

Whether similar findings would be obtained from a comparative study carried out in this country is difficult to say because of the almost complete absence of 'structured' programmes in nursery centres in England. Indeed most nursery teachers take the view that we have little to learn from American experience because our own practice is so different. However a study carried out by B. Tizard and Janet Philps (Tizard, Philps and Plewis, 1976) suggests that what Miller and Dyer found to be true in Kentucky may be equally true in England.

In this study as reported by Barbara Tizard (1975a) in her SSRC review of British pre-school education,

observations on staff behaviour were made in 12 different pre-school centres. Four were nurseries rather than schools, and the staff, who were not teachers, disclaimed any educational aim; four were traditional nursery schools, and four were nursery schools which had departed from tradition to the extent of including a special language programme in the school day. In half of the centres most of the children had parents in the manual working-classes, whilst in the other half the parents of the children were predominantly from the professional middle-classes. . . .

The results show that significant differences did occur in staff behaviour in the various types of centres. In those nursery schools where a language programme was used the staff spent more time interacting with the children, rather than merely supervising them or putting out play equipment. In the nursery centres which had no avowed educational aim there was least talk addressed to children, the lowest amount of information was given, the fewest suggestions for activities were made, and the least time was spent explaining or showing children how to do things. Further, all types of 'cognitive' staff behaviour, as well as total amount of talk to children, were observed more often in middle-class than working-class centres, whilst in working-class centres the staff spent more time putting out equipment and merely supervising the children. Thus, the greatest 'cognitive' content in staff behaviour was found in the middle-class schools with a language programme, the least in the working-class nurseries not staffed by teachers.

Ecological intervention

We have mentioned that one reason why the Milwaukee Project may have been so successful was that the children spent so much time in the nursery centre that it constituted in effect a second home for them. This point has been taken up and elaborated by Bronfenbrenner (1975) who has analysed the findings of the major studies and attempted to synthesise them. Bronfenbrenner's conclusion is that we cannot expect the school to compensate for the effects of an adverse home environment even if it has an effective programme for young disadvantaged children and follows this with an equally well-chosen curriculum for older pupils. Anything the school does leaves out the other half of the child's world — his home environment. An analysis of programmes which have effectively involved and worked through parents rather than children leads him to conclude that whereas intervention which is confined to activity centred on children in an institutional setting — nursery or school — makes at best only a modest contribution to the developmental competence of the disadvantaged, programmes which also involve parents have a much more positive outcome. A combination of nursery centre and home-based programme might offer the best of both.

Bronfenbrenner does not, as some others have done, recommend that school-based programmes should simply be scrapped in favour of home visiting schemes. Rather, he makes far-reaching proposals quite similar to many of those we ourselves have touched upon, for what he calls ecological intervention. The purpose of this would be to transform the conditions of life for disadvantaged families in ways that would enable them to provide good care for their children. This they cannot do if they are overcrowded, poor, grossly overworked, sick, and ignorant. A first need is therefore to provide the family with adequate health care, nutrition,

202

housing and employment. Without such changes, he says, direct forms of intervention such as home visits, pre-school programmes or both, can have little impact on the most deprived families, whose children stand in greatest need of help.

Bronfenbrenner makes recommendations as to the kinds of far-reaching social changes that are needed to offset the glaring inequalities and injustices of society which bear so hard upon children. Some of these (relating to employment and housing for example) raise major problems of social policy. Others focus more specifically upon the needs of families living in the unjust world of today and no doubt tomorrow. In Britain these latter needs are served by the health visiting and paediatric service, and the services provided by local education authorities and local authority social services departments. None of these are very effective today; but improvements may follow the reports of the Court Committee (an official committee under the chairmanship of Professor Donald Court which is considering the future of the child health services) and the Warnock Committee which is examining special education. Because in Britain there is already the institutional basis for comprehensive health and welfare services, marked improvements in their quality and coverage are possible even without major changes in the structure of society, however desirable such changes might be on other grounds.

Bronfenbrenner's case for the importance of parental involvement in early child programmes if the effects are to persist over time raises two sets of questions. The first relates to strategies which would greatly increase the number of ways in which parents could be involved — something we know very little about. One aspect of this is to find ways of encouraging activities in which parents and professionals collaborate. The playgroup movement has given a lead here, and there is no doubt that among the parents of young children there are substantial numbers who have much to offer to early child education and who would wish to participate in a nursery service if they could do so in a meaningful way. There are other adults and young people who would be equally willing to help: at present little use is made of such people.

A second problem arises out of the fact that, as we have pointed out, large numbers of mothers and fathers of young children are working, or are for other reasons unable to participate in nursery services. Others, again for a variety of reasons, do not or cannot modify child-upbringing patterns which, in the eyes of professionals, or other ordinary caring parents, appear dysfunctional, neglectful or harmful. Children of such parents require more than other children — they really do need care which will provide them with the close, affective, one-to-one bonds that are important for social learning and emotional well-being. How to provide these is also a central problem for research (J. Tizard, 1975). The lessons learned in the wartime residential nurseries (see Chapter 10) need to be applied in day care, as in residential nurseries.

Discussion

Any disillusionment there may be about long-term effects of early child education should not be allowed to delay efforts to continue and greatly expand our services in order to meet the pressing short term needs both of young children and their families. There is a continuing need for research, to define groups and permit better assessment of individual children, to devise better educational strategies, and to evaluate their functioning. At present we have hardly begun to know what is effective, for what children, for what families, and why. There is good evidence that various structured programmes do make some difference to the competencies of disadvantaged children however defined; but we know almost nothing about what it is about these that is important. So a great and as yet largely unmet need is to study what actually happens in day care and educational settings and to follow analyses of existing practice with experimental studies designed to change it in ways that promise more rewarding outcomes.

Associated with the need to investigate processes of education and not merely outcomes or products of school experience the nature of which remains unanalysed, we require to develop new indicators both of the way in which children are educated, and of the effects of different patterns of adult-child interaction upon specific aspects of children's behaviour (cf. B. Tizard, Philps and Plewis, 1976).

204

A further point arises out of health service research. In the Thomas Coram Research Unit, Dr Martin Bax and Dr Hilary Hart (to be published) have recently undertaken a detailed history and full paediatric examination of 250 children aged nought to four. The sample constituted 97 per cent of all such children living in a defined geographical area of Bloomsbury, London. The district is by no means a poor inner-city slum; it is particularly well served by hospitals with strong paediatric units; and all children are registered with a general practitioner. In spite of this it was evident that few parents were receiving any help with their children's behavioural problems, and few children were receiving treatment for chronic handicapping conditions of vision, speech, health or development. Thus, 20 per cent of mothers with children over the age of two were worried about their children's speech, and 8 per cent thought they squinted. But these problems had not been referred to a general practitioner or hospital. Likewise, between 5 and 10 per cent of children in the different age groups had marked behaviour problems for which no help had been sought. Medical help was sought for acute illness, but not for chronic problems, or worries, or difficulties of behaviour.

A similar survey is being undertaken in a more socially depressed area of North Paddington: preliminary findings indicate, as would be expected, that the prevalence of untreated, chronic health and behaviour problems is much greater.

Dr Bax and Dr Hart, with June Thomson, an efficient health visitor, have shown that virtually all mothers will bring their children to a child welfare clinic which provides a good service — one that is competent to deal with the child's problems and recognise any that the mothers may have. This means assessment followed by appropriate action.

In this case, in both areas, the child welfare clinic is housed in a day care and education centre to which it can refer children with special needs knowing that these can be met, and in which it can survey and treat the children who attend. Today it is extremely rare to find parents, doctors, health visitors, psychologists, therapists, teachers and child care staff working closely together. The usual pattern, where children do have problems about which anything at all is done, is for them to be referred to a hospital or clinic — which usually has poor communications with people in the environment in which children live. This is both inefficient and expensive. We think that a well-functioning child health clinic housed in a pre-school children's centre would promote the much needed link between paediatrics and child care, and perhaps reduce both the need for hospital treatment and the calls made on general practice.

These and other studies which point in the same direction raise important problems for all nursery education and care. The evidence does suggest strongly that there is a need for a rethinking of the objectives of the nursery curriculum, and of the means by which these can be best achieved. The poor results of existing practice can be seen most clearly in the case of working-class children, but it is probable that our nursery services for all children could be greatly improved.

The implications for the upbringing of young children are twofold. First, for obvious social reasons as well as for the children's own good, we must provide optimal services using the knowledge we have got. Since this is inadequate, and since needs are not uniform, the pattern of services must be encouraged to vary. Secondly, through research both in child development and in the planning, organisation and delivery of services, we must increase our knowledge of the human environment and find ways of using this for benign and noble ends. Many of the major economic and demographic trends we have spoken about appear to be inevitable, in the sense that they are not likely to be averted by planning, by government action or by decisions consciously taken by large numbers of individuals in order to achieve general social ends. But in this context, options are still open to us to determine the kind of society we live in. Insofar as we can state our objectives and the priorities we assign to them, we can work towards ways of attaining them.

No discussion of present and future pre-school provision can avoid making some comment on the problems, adequacy and place of the dominant child-rearing institution in our society — the nuclear family with its sex-based division of roles which make housework and childcare the primary responsibility of the mother.

Our concern arises from the apparent consequences of the way in which family roles are distributed. We have already referred to the very high prevalence of depression among working-class women with young children, and to the widespread dissatisfaction among housewives of all social classes with their lot. Loneliness, often compounded by boredom and a sense of frustration at the lack of stimulation in their lives, are frequent complaints. Increased mobility of families, less contact within extended families and the breaking up of well-established and cohesive communities through rehousing programmes, have exacerbated this loneliness. And boredom and under-stimulation are inherent in a situation where women are left with little more in their lives than an almost exclusive responsibility for domestic tasks and the care of one or two children. Their range of social contacts and activities is limited by their role and the type of work it entails, and many mothers are reduced to isolation or to the society of other mothers.

The role segregation within the nuclear family in our society, and the narrow range of functions it serves, perpetuate many of the current sex inequalities. Even when mothers do paid work there is as a rule no adjustment of roles within the family or of the conditions under which the women are offered employment outside. Hence mothers with young children are too often obliged to do jobs well below their abilities, unskilled jobs that mirror the menial and servicing functions they perform in the household.

We also waste the talents of fathers, who contribute little to the care of either the house or the children. Not only is their contribution missed, but they are denied the satisfaction to be gained from these tasks when they are shared and combined with other activities.

Children are also losers. Many share their mothers' isolation and boredom, and their limited range of activities and environments. Too often it is impossible for mother and child to get away from each other, to find time and space to themselves, to enjoy the variety of relationships and experience that are necessary if their close relationship is not to become cramping.

Viewed in these terms, it is not surprising that there is evidence of considerable stress in families, especially those with young children. In addition to the depression, job dissatisfaction and loneliness of mothers already mentioned, other indicators of stress are abundantly obvious. The incidence of marriage breakdown is increasing rapidly; there is evidence that the quality of many marital relationships deteriorates after the birth of the first child; there is a growing awareness of the violence within the family, both inflicted by parents on children and by parents on one another (though whether this is increasing, as is often said, is uncertain); and disturbed behaviour is by no means uncommon among young children. Signs of these strains can be seen in all social classes. Thus a recent study of 500 homes in a private housing estate, where 78 per cent of the men worked as executives, reported many of the same problems as have been found in other social groups, sometimes in an even more acute form. Sex-role divisions within the families were particularly sharp and many recent assumptions about trends to greater equality within middle-class marriages were shown to be largely myth. Husbands, commuting many miles to their jobs and working long hours in furtherance of careers, were away from home for substantial periods of time, making much participation by them in child-rearing impossible; many did not even see their children awake during the week.

Nearly all the routine decisions about child and home had to be taken by the wives alone; and in the absence of the emotional and practical support expected of men in middle-class families, the wives fell back on other isolated wives on the estate for support (*Sunday Times* report, 31 August 1975, of a paper given by Dr Gaynor Cohen at the British Association).

A more personalised account of the middle-class experience is given in an article on the pleasures and anxieties of motherhood by Margaret Drabble (cited in Holt, 1975):

> Small children — toddlers, as they are rather offensively labelled — are well known to be extremely exhausting. . . . I think now that the pleasures of that time are outweighed by the pains, though naturally I didn't think so at the time; but looking back, I wonder how I endured it. One is programmed to endure the most terrible things. And at this stage I must admit that an addiction to children is accompanied by the most frightful and serious disadvantages. It is all very well to recall the good moments, but what about all the bad times, the exhaustion, the illnesses, the bad temper and, worst of all, the endless, sickening anxiety? On the most profound level, once one has had children one can never be carefree again; each pleasure is snatched from the grave. They are hostages to fortune. I used to be a reasonably careless and adventurous person, before I had children; now I am morbidly obsessed by seat belts and constantly afraid that low-flying aircraft will drop on my children's school,

John Holt's comment on this lament is equally relevant:

> The woman speaking here is not poor; she does the work she likes best; and she is competent, admired and successful in this work. If this is how she feels about having children, how must all those women feel who are pressed by poverty, or at least by worries about money and who, in factory, shop or home do drudge work for little money or none at all?

The social and demographic changes discussed in the introductory chapter have probably placed the family under growing pressure, while ideological developments — such as the

questioning and criticisms levelled by the women's movement — have increased consciousness of dissatisfaction and
oppression. It is difficult to know whether the quality of life
for women with young children has deteriorated, and if so, in
what ways. But we do know that for large numbers of them
today life is unsatisfying. There is no doubt either that many
families with young children suffer added stress from low
income, unsatisfactory housing and the impact of grossly
deprived inner-city and other environments.

It would be unrealistic to expect educational and day-care
services for young children to make more than a limited,
though highly important, contribution to the happiness and
wellbeing of young children and their families. As we see it,
an adequate child care policy would be part of a more comprehensive *family* policy, and this would be designed to raise
the status of women; to strengthen the bonds that bind family
members together; to increase the choice open to parents
about how they organise their lives in general and their child-
rearing in particular; and to improve the quality of life of
parents and children. Within this context, one aim of family
policy should be to facilitate and encourage greater role-
sharing between men and women within the family.

Recently the whole question of greater equality within
the family, and ways of achieving this, has become a matter
of serious debate in some countries. In September 1975, a
Council of Europe conference for European Ministers responsible for family affairs was held in Oslo to discuss the implications for government action on family policy of the growing
equality of women. The development of the 'symmetrical
family', where both partners have absolute equality, was a
major theme of the conference.

The Norwegian government believes that equality *within* the
family is the essential precondition for equality in all other
fields. Unless men and women are prepared, indeed,
enabled, to share all family responsibilities from bread-
winning to child care and household tasks, little will
change.

Women will continue to spend years at home caring for
husband, children and home with the prospect of a poorly

paid, low status job when the children are older. Men will go on being excluded from the major part of the caring of their own children and be expected to work throughout their lives to provide the family with its income.

Scandinavian countries are attempting to change those roles by helping parents to share their responsibilities, at least while the children are small, by altering employment conditions, social security and child care facilities. The emphasis is very much on giving people a real choice over whether they want to remain at home full-time; pursue a career, or combine jobs with family responsibilities.

In Sweden, for example, maternity benefits were replaced last year by 'parent's insurance' giving a right to seven months leave after the birth of a child. Either parent can take the leave, or they can share it in whatever proportions they choose. . . . The Norwegians suggest that parents of very young children should have the right to a six-hour day with compensation for loss of earnings through taxation or social security.

'We must get away from the attitude that children are primarily the responsibility of the mother', Mrs Valle (Norwegian Minister of Justice) said. 'Children are the responsibility and joy of both parents.'

Although trade unions, employers and government in Britain have scarcely begun to press for the reforms which would bring about such changes in patterns of work and lifestyle, the British Minister at the Oslo conference told the other delegates

'the aim should not be to force both husband and wife to work outside the home and share duties within it. It should be to create the conditions necessary to enable a couple to make a completely free decision, uninfluenced by any constraints whether legislative, administrative or financial.'

Where couples did choose to share responsibilities completely, the purpose of government was to identify possible stress points and to plan to meet the resulting needs of families (Reports from *The Times*, 19 September 1975 and 3 October 1975).

A complement to new employment patterns would be new

and different patterns of family allowance designed to ensure that, where man and wife shared domestic commitments as well as paid work outside the home, they were not at a financial disadvantage in consequence. If there was a child-care allowance for families with only one wage-earner, then a proportion of this allowance might be paid to families with two role-sharing parents, each employed part-time.

To make this possible would require changes and improvements in the opportunities made available to women to learn marketable work skills.

> One of the main recommendations of Lady Seear's report, 'Re-entry of Women to the Labour Market after Interruption of Employment', was for counselling and vocational guidance to prevent women from automatically gravitating back to the recognisable but lower-paid women's jobs. She also recommended special training arrangements to correct the built-in biases in the education of girls . . . . Flexible training arrangements will also be an important contribution. By 'flexible' we mean arrangements which take account of women's current responsibilities. In Sweden the state not only makes courses available, but will also pay for family welfare at home when the mother is attending training courses. In Canada, allowances for retraining are available for women who are still at home but wish to return to work (Nandy and Nandy, 1975).

A greater sharing of roles could help overcome some of the problems at present experienced in families, especially by mothers. However, in many families, certainly in the immediate future, one parent, usually the mother, will choose to stay at home and take responsibility for child care and housework, leaving the other parent free to undertake full-time employment. As we have already stressed, policies and services should enable parents who prefer to make such a choice not to be disadvantaged as a consequence. Parents who wish to take it in turns to stay at home full-time should be similarly helped. A child-care allowance for families with less than two full-time wage earners is an obvious means of support, just as it would be to role-sharing parents each employed only part-time. Such an allowance, while benefiting many families where the mother is not at work or where she works from sheer financial necessity, is unlikely to lead to a large-scale reduction in the numbers of employed mothers, since as we have already discussed, many work for other than purely financial reasons.

We could however try to ensure that parents who work full-time at childcare or housework do not become socially segregated as a result. By this, we mean that they should not be inevitably cut off from social relationships, activities and opportunities which having responsibility for young children may make it hard for them to participate in. The whole question of social segregation of mothers with young children — the sense of loneliness, of being cut off from the wider world and former interests by the constant demands of childcare — is in some respects analogous with that of the social segregation of handicapped people, who also have suffered though to a more marked degree, from an inability to participate fully in the life of the community. In both cases, 'special' activity groups or organisations, be they for mothers or disabled people, may be preferable to there being no opportunities for social activities at all; but while such groups may always have a limited function, meaningful integration into mixed groups, environments and activities provides a more socially desirable objective.

Steps such as these form part of a comprehensive and coherent policy to help meet the needs and problems of young families. And such a policy would concern itself also with housing, employment, income, transport, education and training, and other matters which we do not discuss here. The present lack of coherence in policy is abundantly clear in general — and results specifically in the irrational fragmentation and inequity of pre-school services.

Obviously the development of pre-school provision makes best sense as part of a comprehensive reappraisal of the whole issue of child-rearing and family relations. However, even without this, it is possible to describe some guidelines for the development of a popular and effective pre-school service.

1   *The service should be local.* In urban areas at least,

pre-school services should normally be within walking distance of the home — the sort of walking distance that is feasible with two small children in tow. This means not having to cross busy roads, or to walk very far. If each pre-school centre served a small catchment area most of the children who came to it would live near by.

2 *The service should be free.* One of the most discriminatory anomalies of the present service is that nursery education is free while parental contributions are expected of playgroup and day nursery users, the former paying a flat rate, the latter according to their means. For a society which provides free education, including free higher education, and a free child health service, a free pre-school service is a logical corollary.

3 *The service should be planned and supervised by one authority.* Both nationally and locally, the present division of responsibility between social services and education authorities makes little sense. Not only is the division difficult to justify, but it perpetuates anomalies of payment, availability and placement. At present welfare services are highly selective, being designed for the deviant and deprived, whereas education services are in principle available to all sectors of the community. The present situation makes coordinated planning virtually impossible.

The need for the education and care of young children to be the overall responsibility of one authority at national and local level seems clear. Whether education or social services authorities are eventually chosen for this responsibility, the responsibility must embrace children from birth onwards and cover education and care throughout the day and year — not just during school hours and terms.

However, planning and supervision by one statutory agency does not mean that this agency must itself actually supply all services. Many other Western European countries, for example, give much more support from public funds than we do to voluntary agencies which provide day care. A substantial proportion of public funds for pre-school services might be used to finance voluntary provision; indeed voluntary centres might be entitled to public funds for both capital and running costs provided they met certain criteria and standards, such as those outlined here. This could lead for instance to the growth of

214

nursery centres initiated by communities or parents, a few of which have recently opened in London, for example the Children's Community Centre in Camden (Children's Community Centre, 1974, unpublished). The playgroup movement could also play a role in such development of voluntary services, if it was prepared to develop to meet a wider range of needs and demands than it does at present.

The actual balance between statutory and voluntary provision under the designated supervising authority for pre-school services remains to be worked out, but the contribution of both types of provision is as essential to future services as unity of overall responsibility.

4 *The service should be organised so that children are not allocated services simply according to their family's social need or the hours required.* The present hotch-potch of pre-school provision (day nurseries, factory nurseries, nursery schools, nursery classes, reception classes, playgroups, minders) and the distribution of children among them, reflect a mixture of historical accident — the needs (of parents especially) for particular hours of care, the local availability of services and the criteria of admission. The needs of the child rarely figure. Each type of service has its own set of hours, not normally adjusted to the needs of parents and child. We require a much greater integration of services; if diversity remains it should be on the basis not of hours and age, but of philosophy and attitudes so that it offers parents within a locality a real choice. We should, in short, have fewer types of service but greater variety of services within multi-purpose local centres. Day nurseries and nursery schools illustrate the social segregation that occurs when services are neither locally based nor multi-purpose. Three and four year old children, with similar educational and social needs, are distributed between these two services — each with its own type of staff, orientation and objectives — because the needs, and usually the social circumstances, of their parents differ. As a consequence, the most deprived children are to be found in day nurseries while more advantaged children receive nursery education.

5 *The service should provide a wide range of functions and be available to parents on demand.* Greater integration of

services should not mean greater uniformity in services offered. A centre providing for those needs at present met by playgroups, day nurseries and nursery schools, must be able to offer a range of hours — from two to nine hours a day — and all-year opening, at least five days a week. The main aim of an integrated pre-school centre should be to offer high quality care for young children in its catchment area, at the age and, within reason, for the hours that their parents want. The service must therefore be available to all families, and not selective in its intake, and must be based on demand, not need.

A centre for day-care and education might also offer a range of other services to young families living locally, even perhaps to the local community as a whole. For example a welfare clinic; a toy and book library; clothes-washing facilities (if these are not readily available elsewhere); a meeting place for local groups; a food cooperative.

6 *Health is important too.* Our own studies in the Thomas Coram Research Unit as well as other epidemiological surveys have shown that there is a high incidence of untreated medical and behavioural pathology among young children. In general, parents take their children to the family doctor for acute illnesses, but they fail to consult him for chronic problems of developmental delay or dysfunction, or seek advice for behavioural problems which are a major cause of concern. There are good reasons for this. Most doctors are not 'interested' in developmental problems, and the advice they give is not well informed. The public health and infant welfare centres have not been a great success because their functions have been largely diagnostic and advisory — the doctors could not prescribe for medical conditions, and could only refer children with psychological disorders, or in need of speech therapy, physiotherapy or psychotherapy, to a hospital or clinic, or recommend placement in a nursery. In day nurseries and nursery schools the medical role has been largely one of inspection: there is little day-to-day contact between community paediatricians and nursery staff.

The reorganisation of the National Health Service does at least offer the opportunity to unify primary care and community medicine for children. This can only come about if nursery centres have a paediatrician who visits them regularly and frequently, and who concerns himself with treatment as well as assessment. The need for this is clear enough. What we lack at present are doctors who have the time *and the skills* to work in this way.

As for psychological services for young children, they are almost non-existent. The few child psychologists in paediatric and psychiatric units who see many young children are almost all in assessment units, and educational psychologists as a rule spend very little time with children under compulsory school age. Again the shortages are of time and of skills; and as with the doctors so with the psychologists. The structure of local authority services, and the traditional definition of professional roles, prevent effective services from developing.

How these problems are to be resolved we do not know. But if nursery centres are to provide really adequate care for young children, they must have easy access to specialist health and psychological services which must be closely involved in what goes on in the centres, not just concerned with children who visit clinics.

As a matter of course those concerned with the health and wellbeing of young children in nurseries must also be in contact with their parents. Probably the most successful way of doing so is through the establishment of an infant welfare or child-health clinic at the centre itself.

7   *Collaboration between parents and professionals.* A nursery centre will only be effective if it meets the needs and wishes of the parents. Many parents have a strong desire to share in the care of young children in an organised way, as the phenomenal success of playgroups, and the enthusiasm of those who take part in them, indicates. In day nurseries and even nursery schools this desire remains largely unfulfilled. Parents do not as a rule take a significant part in the day-to-day work of the nursery. Instead, the professional training of nurses and teachers fosters the belief that nursery care is really a job for professionals. (That is why the playgroup movement, which disputed this, was greeted with some hostility by professional organisations.) We have yet to work out satisfactory institutional structures which would promote and sustain effective collaboration among professional staff and parents (and other volunteers). Until we do this, the important ingredient

'working with parents' will not be seen as an essential part of all staff training and all nursery practice.

Working with parents does not mean simply helping mothers with their difficulties, or holding mothers' classes. It should mean enlisting the active participation of parents in the day-to-day life of the nursery, learning from as well as teaching them, working together. To learn how to do this is perhaps the hardest skill for professional people to learn and practise: yet without this partnership the nursery is impoverished, and will always be short-staffed.

As we point out later on, parent participation in nurseries involves complex problems of definition and relationships. These need study and discussion, but the principle remains, that parents must play a much larger part than they do today in the formulation of nursery goals and in the care and education of young children in nursery care, if the services are to function effectively and provide places for all young children whose families wish them to attend.

8   *The staffing of the service should be broad-based and flexible.* Pre-school services need to draw more widely, for their *paid* workers, on two groups in the community with much potentially to offer: young men, and middle-aged and older people of both sexes, especially those with experience of raising their own families. Apart from the reserves of talent and experience in these two groups, largely untapped at present, the current female monopoly of staffing, especially with so many younger women employed, reinforces the limited range of adult relationships that young children are increasingly faced with. To encourage the recruitment of middle-aged men and women, but also because it is not clear that existing training is necessarily the best we could have, more emphasis should be put on in-service training and less on longer, general courses. Greater integration of existing services, and of the agencies responsible for them, will require a more rational system of staffing, with a rethink in particular of the existing dichotomy between nursery nurses and teachers. Current attempts to integrate day nursery and nursery school services within one centre too often lead to the establishment of what are in practice separate day nursery and nursery school units, each with its own groups of staff, linked only

218

through sharing a common site. This is not what we mean by an integrated and multi-purpose children's centre. However the distinction between nursery nurses and teachers — for instance over status and work conditions — impedes the setting up of a genuinely integrated service in which all needs are met by one group of staff in a multi-purpose neighbourhood centre.

These eight guidelines would lead us to new patterns of nursery service. But the list is not a complete one, and a number of other issues need resolving. Among these are the following:

1 *Choice:* How far can or should parents be offered a choice of provision? Of particular relevance in this issue is the relative contribution to be made by voluntary and statutory provision. How far should resources be put into developing services provided directly by statutory agencies and how far into stimulating community and other voluntary initiatives?

2 *Provision for children under three:* Official hostility to the idea of day care for children under three and a parallel belief that parental interest in, and children's readiness for, part-time provision increases at three, has meant that little serious thought has been given to meeting the full-time and part-time needs and demands of families with very young children. We do not even know how many children under three are receiving such services at present and where they are, though we do know that most of those receiving more than part-time care will be with child minders. The need for provision for this group requires to be accepted. However, much more careful consideration must be given to the manner in which their needs are met — what is the most appropriate scale and size of the provision to be made for them? Can or should converted domestic accommodation be used? Should their provision be separate from or with that for older children? What about staffing and the actual content of the service? What part-time provision is needed for under threes attending both with and without parents? What contribution should or can child minders make?

3 *Why five?* In all the recent discussion about pre-school provision, the great divide between children of compulsory school age and 'pre-school' children has remained largely

unchallenged. At five, or in some cases 'rising five' all children suddenly become entitled to free, full (school) day provision; one national and local agency assumes responsibility for their care in the day. Of course, not all children necessarily gain from this transition — the child, for instance, who at four is at day nursery, where she receives all-day, all-year care, at five is in school which only offers school hours and school terms. In the past at least, the education system has not been marked by great flexibility or initiative in this respect.

Views on school starting age have varied with the years. At the beginning of the nineteenth century, six or seven was held to be an appropriate age to begin formal education; but by the end of the century, though five had been somewhat arbitrarily selected as the compulsory starting age, many three and four year olds went to elementary schools. At the present time, increasing numbers of three and four year olds are attending primary schools, either in nursery or reception classes, though five still retains its official significance.

A more integrated service for children under five, under the auspices of a single authority, and a willingness to make education services accept responsibility for the day-care needs of older children, would bring the question 'why five?' into even sharper focus. Why not birth to seven or eight, or birth to two and three to eight as dividing points in the organisation of the education service, irrespective of whether five remains as the age of compulsory schooling? With such issues left unresolved, no definitive recommendations for the reorganisation of pre-school provision can be made.

Our criteria suggest that the basic form of service should be through multi-purpose children's centres offering part and full-time care with medical and other services, to a very local catchment area, but there is much room for experimentation involving different age groupings of children; for example, from birth to two years, then a new grouping from three to four or three to seven; or one grouping from birth to four or even from birth to seven; different sizes of centres (from 10 to 60 or 70 places); purpose-built or domestic accommodation; different methods of management, for example, local authority, voluntary organisation, community

220

group. We ourselves are associated with the development of two such multi-purpose, integrated centres — the Thomas Coram Children's Centre (Director, Rita Marchant) in Bloomsbury, and the Dorothy Gardner Children's Centre (Principal, Ethel Roberts) in Paddington; they are exploring in practice many of the issues touched upon in this book. At the time of writing the centres were not fully established and functioning, and a report on their progress is thus a matter for the future. However, the need for further curriculum research and for a serious study to be made of staffing, and of costs, is very evident.

4 What contribution can child minders make? The situation of some minded children, and the wide extent of unregistered child minding, have given rise to much concern and adverse publicity. But at the same time, using minders in the expansion of public day-care services has attracted considerable support, both in Britian and abroad, normally in association with proposals for varying degrees of involvement by public authorities in training, recruitment and direct payment of minders. Publicly subsidised systems of minding — often referred to as family day care or day fostering — have been introduced to some extent in most Western countries and a number of British local authorities are developing such schemes, as well as training and support schemes for minders continuing to operate in the purely private day-care market.

The arguments for using child minders to expand public day care are essentially that they are cheaper (especially on capital costs), easier and faster to develop, and generally more flexible than day nurseries. Above all, they are supposed to offer a more appropriate type of care, especially for children under two or three years, by providing more individualised and stable care in a more   homelike environment. The case for this type of provision has been put most clearly by the Finer Committee who argued that, while there was a need for more day care:

It would not be desirable for expansion to be channelled primarily through day nurseries and to ensure that day care services are adequate it will be necessary to increase non-institutional services . . . . We believe that for the children of working mothers, and particularly where mothers work full time, local authorities should be encouraged to develop comprehensive day fostering (ie. a child minding scheme in which minders are employed and paid by local authorities) . . . . This kind of home-based device can offer the child the care which is nearest to that which parents usually provide.

Central to their thinking was a belief in the importance to the very young child of a regular mother substitute and that minders could better provide this than day nurseries.

So far we have said little about child minders, because we know little about them. Little study has been made of how they might be trained or supervised; how many good minders could be recruited and at what cost; the difference for children of care in good nurseries and minding situations; and what actually happens in the minding situation, and how often and in what circumstances it does approximate to the normal home and family situation. Up to now, for instance, the argument that child minding should be preferred as a form of care because it comes as near as one can get to care in a good family is based on mere assertion. We are by no means convinced by it. Our experience, although based on few cases, is that even registered minders who are well spoken of by local authority workers do not on the whole offer a continuous, warm and individualised relationship with their charges. Nor do they stimulate their children intellectually. More generally, turnover of children and minders appears to be considerable, though here as with so much else in this subject we must rely on impressions rather than systematic data.

The more extensive information gathered by the Thomas Coram Research Unit on parental preference for pre-school provision shows that very few mothers would choose to send a young child to a child minder if a day care centre were available instead — though of course if all child minders were properly trained and supervised opinions might change.

We know of no adequate study of costs of a high quality day-fostering programme, with minders properly paid, trained, housed and equipped, covered for illness and holiday, and

222

extensively supported and supervised; no doubt minders' capital costs should be less than those of a day nursery, but the difference in running costs might not be much. Furthermore, the use of converted domestic accommodation to establish small, community-run nurseries, employing local men and women, could also reduce the capital cost differential. Indeed until local authorities are willing to experiment with alternative forms of day care, smaller and less formal than day nurseries, and drawing on the good features of minders and nurseries, the direction day-care developments should take will remain unclear.

The day-fostering projects being introduced by some local authorities at present could help to answer some of the questions posed in this section, and it may turn out that minding should and could play an extensive role in public day care services. But as we have made clear, we see great problems at present in proposals that child minding should play more than a quite minor part in a comprehensive nursery service, especially if made at the expense of other innovations in day care. Considering the urgent need to develop a policy on day care, the large number of children at present minded, and the strong parental unease about much of it, there is clearly a need for much more investigation. Our present ignorance is truly deplorable.

5 *Parent involvement:* We have put parent involvement among our eight 'guidelines' for good nursery practice; but how collaboration between parents and professionals can best be fostered raises many unresolved questions.

First, the term itself needs clarification, since it is used to mean many different things. Parental involvement can, for instance, be used to cover such diverse activities as fund-raising; or 'parent power' through control of management and administration, for example through selection of staff and dictation of the aims and methods; or encouraging parents to visit a nursery in order to observe what goes on and see their children in a different setting; or including both child and parent in a joint learning programme aimed perhaps at modifying behaviour; or parents helping paid staff in a variety of ways in the actual nursery, even to the extent of supplying the bulk of all labour required to run the service. This is not an exhaustive list but the answers to the questions posed below will depend on which type of parental involvement is being considered.

Secondly, we should ask ourselves why we think parent involvement so important. It may be that parental involvement through help with running a service is essential to its survival — many playgroups, especially in the early days of the movement, are examples of this. A more political argument being raised at present in Scandinavian countries, and in the United States, is that parents should not leave decisions on educational matters to professionals, but should exert a measure of control over methods and aims. At the opposite pole to this essentially 'parent power' view, is one often implicit, but sometimes made explicit, in discussions among professionals of parental involvement. Many believe that it will help parents to be better parents, more competent in their dealings with their children, if they can be taught what to do by professionals. This implies that the models of behaviour with children offered by the professionals are relevant and beneficial to parents. A further assumption often made is that it is working-class parents who are in particular need of this type of instruction, being more ignorant and less capable of meeting the needs of their children than middle-class parents. This view is based on the belief in a need to effect change in the parents if significant progress is to be made with the child, and so acknowledges the prime influence of the home on the child. Bronfenbrenner's (1974) review of the long-term outcome of Head Start studies, which suggested to him that only in those in which parents were actively involved could any discernible long term benefit to the children be demonstrated, supports this view about the primacy of the home. The evidence is, however, largely retrospective and interpretive, and it is by no means certain how widely generalisable it is.

Thirdly, we should try to find out more about how much — and how many — parents want to be involved in the education and day care of their own and others' children. Because there is no hard evidence on this, we must again speculate. That a proportion of parents want to be actively involved in helping in services has been shown by the success of the playgroup movement, though even here the requirement to

224

help as a condition for a place makes it difficult to assess how many parents would freely choose to help on duty rotas, and with administration and fund-raising. For other parents the demands of employment, other children and other interests all limit the time, energy and enthusiasm available for pre-school services. A third group of parents would not wish to be involved anyhow, except in a very peripheral way. We do not know the numbers of parents likely to fall into these and other categories. It is also not clear how far interest in involvement varies between mothers and fathers; in many cases what is meant by parental involvement is really mothers' involvement — the number of fathers for instance taking their turn on playgroup rotas is probably very small.

Fourthly, what actually happens when parents are involved? At present we know very little about what parental involvement of any sort there is, or of what actually goes on when parents are involved. To take playgroups again as an example, the movement has clearly involved many parents, mainly mothers, in a number of ways, including actually helping with the children. However there has been no study of what parents are expected to do, or actually do when they help, or of the effect of the increasing number of trained, paid playgroup leaders on this involvement. How often has the introduction of professional workers into this type of provision led to changing patterns of parental activity?

A fifth issue is the way in which professionals react to parental involvement. Again the type of involvement is likely to be crucial — a centre where parents hire and fire, and one where staff are responsible to a local authority, is likely to produce both different professional-parent relationships and different professional attitudes. However, the attitudes of professional workers to parents vary a good deal, and we know little about why this is or how to change unfavourable stereotypes.

Most of these questions must remain unanswered until we have more experience of different types of involvement in operation and have made much more study of them. But a few general points can be made. Any effective pre-school service must be responsive to the needs, wishes and experience of its parents, a proportion of whom will wish to be

225

involved in a variety of ways, from fund-raising to running the centre. Given encouragement, an increasing number will probably wish to be involved in the discussion and shaping of aims and methods — and the issue of parent power will become more pressing in the future. Because parents have, and must have, the primary responsibility for their children, and because child care is such a highly labour-intensive industry, parental involvement in nursery centres is very necessary. But how best to achieve it is not at all clear.

All the issues raised here require study, experiment and discussion. But to undertake this implies a readiness to admit the need to review and change the well-established forms of provision on which future developments have been planned. Today's services are not simply inadequate in quantity; they are also fragmented and unresponsive to changing needs. One of the few benefits of the present bleak economic climate is that it may offer a chance to review existing policies, experiment with new options and work out better policies not just for pre-school services but for families with young children also.

Appendix: Tables

1: Growth of population of England and Wales
2: Under-fives in maintained primary schools (England and Wales) since 1947
3: Maintained nursery schools since 1946 (England and Wales)
4: Day nurseries, private nurseries and child minders in England and Wales, 1945 — 1974
5: Age distribution of pupils under five in maintained primary schools (England and Wales)
6: Age distribution of pupils in maintained nursery schools (England and Wales)
7: Employment rates of mothers of pre-school children in seven countries
8: Employment rates of mothers with pre-school children in various local authority areas

1: Growth of population of England and Wales

Year	Total population (millions)	Population under five (millions)
1086	1.5	
1695	5.5	
1801	9.0	
1841	16.0	2.1
1851	18.0	2.4
1871	22.7	3.1
1891	29.0	3.6
1911	35.0	3.9
1953	44.0	
1973	49.0	3.7

Sources: McKeown 1965; Censuses; Registrar General

2: Under-fives in maintained primary schools (England and Wales) since 1947

Year	Pupils			Total places (part-time pupils counted as half)	Total pupils as % of age group 2-4 years
	Full-time	Part-time	Total		
1947	184,697		184,697	184,697	9.4
1948	179,275		179,275		
1949	170,715		170,715		
1950	148,428		148,428	148,428	6.6
1953	150,033		150,033		
1955	152,790	1,000	153,790	153,290	7.8
1956	156,017	1,100	157,117		
1960	174,910	1,703	176,613	175,761	8.7
1961	180,874	2,730	183,604		
1962	190,581	3,929	194,510		
1963	180,241	5,914	186,155		
1964	182,351	7,421	189,772		
1965	197,476	10,431	207,907	202,691	8.7
1966	197,829	11,382	209,211		
1967	197,520	13,876	211,397		
1968	209,953	16,857	226,810		9.0
1969	220,473	22,778	243,251		9.6
1970	228,292	28,520	256,812	242,552	10.4
1971	244,821	37,453	282,374		11.6
1972	263,805	48,154	311,959		13.2
1973	291,579	59,660	351,239	321,409	15.2

Sources: Ministry of Education Annual Reports 1947 and 1949; Statistics of Education (Department of Education annual publication) HMSO.
Table of part-time pupils given in 1973 Statistics, confirmed as under-fives by cross reference to other volumes of the Statistics.

3: Maintained nursery schools since 1946 (England and Wales)

Year	Schools	Full-time pupils	Part-time pupils	Total	Total as % children aged 2-4 years	Total places (part-time pupils counted as half)
1946	75	6,000	–	6,000		
1947	353	18,173	–	18,173	0.9	18,173
1948	398	20,343	–	20,343		
1949	412	21,003	–	21,003		
1950	416	21,079	–	21,079	0.9	21,079
1951	434	21,735	–	21,735		
1952	457	22,464	–	22,464		
1953	453	22,672	–	22,672		
1954	457	22,636	–	22,636		
1955	464	23,127	–	23,127	1.2	23,127
1956	465	23,322	–	23,322		
1957	460	22,934	–	22,934		
1958	457	22,193	978	23,171		
1959	454	21,746	1,659	23,405		
1960	454	21,757	2,239	23,996	1.2	22,876
1961	453	21,319	2,981	24,300		
1962	455	20,881	4,388	25,269		
1963	458	20,504	5,539	26,043		
1964	460	20,580	6,184	26,764		
1965	461	19,927	7,975	27,902	1.2	23,914
1966	462	19,417	9,044	28,461		
1967	464	19,039	10,385	29,424		
1968	467	17,957	12,716	30,673		
1969	470	17,170	15,070	32,240		
1970	482	16,441	17,779	34,220	1.4	25,330
1971	498	15,596	20,718	36,314	1.3	
1972	527	15,443	23,998	39,441	1.7	
1973	548	15,450	26,947	42,397	1.8	28,923

Source: Adapted from Table C, Statistics of Education,
Vol. 1, 1973.

4: Day nurseries, private nurseries and child minders in England and Wales, 1945-1974

YEAR	DAY NURSERIES		PRIVATE NURSERIES			CHILD MINDERS		
	No. of places	% popu-lation aged 0-5 yrs	No.	No. of children	% popu-lation aged 0-5	No.	No. of child-ren	% pop-ula-tion aged 0-5 yrs
1945	1,300	62,784	–	–		–	–	
1946	914	43,618	–	–		–	–	
1947	902	42,365	–	–		–	–	
1948	882	41,065	–	–		–	–	
1949	910	43,395	250	6,893		271	1,703	
1950	884	42,410	326	8,965		415	2,638	
1951	832	40,410	1.1 / 339	9,872	0.3	468	3,506	0.1
1952	797	38,078	373	10,316		560	4,178	
1953	724	34,705	391	10,773		638	4,737	
1954	628	30,091	413	11,296		715	5,570	
1955	583	28,024	443	11,679		777	6,090	
1956	547	26,109	464	12,018		881	6,964	
1957	526	25,014	496	12,543		949	7,536	
1958	501	23,676	544	13,352		1,138	8,981	
1959	486	23,048	543	13,155		1,313	10,192	
1960	477	22,564	601	14,595		1,531	11,881	
1961	472	22,259	0.6 / 747	17,618	0.5	1,780	13,999	0.4
1962	462	21,876	932	22,591		2,202	17,600	
1963	459	21,672	1,243	31,045		2,597	20,800	
1964	455	21,532	1,585	38,144		2,994	24,000	
1965	448	21,396	2,245	55,543		3,393	27,200	
1966	445	21,157	0.5 / 3,083	75,132	1.8	3,887	32,336	0.8
1967	444	21,169	4,382	109,141		5,039	42,696	
1968	445	21,163	5,849	146,098		5,802	47,208	
1969	444	21,142	8,467	203,093		18,168	70,531	
1970	453	21,581	0.5 / 10,043	248,883	6.2	25,595	84,861	2.1
1971								
1972	467	22,580	0.6 / 11,924	295,960	7.7	29,191	90,036	2.4
1973	493	23,838	0.6 / 13,397	335,332	9.0	30,333	91,878	2.5
1974	517	24,772	14,843	362,320		30,552	86,954	

Sources: Yudkin (1967) to 1965; DHSS Annual reports 1966 to 1970; No figures for 1971; Health & Personal Social Service Statistics for 1972; Local Authority annual returns for 1973.

5: Age distribution of pupils under five in maintained primary schools (England and Wales)

Year	Aged 2 No.	%	Aged 3 No.	%	Aged 4 No.	%	Aged 4 (rising 5) No.	%	Total No.	%
1947	953	0.5	32,437	17.5	151,310	82%			184,700	100
1953	89	-	13,199	9.0	136,746	91%			150,034	100
1965	208	-	9,967	5.0	67,861	34.5	119,440	60.5	197,476*	100
1973	739	-	33,327	9.5	146,093	41.5	171,080	49.0	351,239	100

*Does not include 10,431 part-time pupils

Sources: Yudkin 1967; Statistics of Education HMSO.

6: Age distribution of pupils in maintained nursery schools (England and Wales)

Year	Aged 2 No.	%	Aged 3 No.	%	Aged 4 No.	%	Total No.	%
1947	3,794	21.5	7,169	40.5	6,780	38.0	17,743	100
1953	2,924	13.0	8,813	40.0	10,379	47.0	22,116	100
1966	1,652	7.0	10,123	43.0	11,872	50.0	23,647	100
1973	2,002	5.0	21,041	50.0	19,104*	45.0	42,147	100

*1,342 of these were rising five

Sources: Ministry of Education Annual reports; Statistics of Education, HMSO.

7: Employment rates of mothers of pre-school children in seven countries

Country	Age range of children	Employment rate of mothers				
		Rate	Year	Rate	Year	Change in rate
Austria	0 – 5	-	-	26.7%	1971	-
Britain	0 – 4	11.5%	1961	18.7%	1971	+ 65%
Germany	0 – 5	31.3%	1961	31.2%	1970	No change
Netherlands	0 – 3	-	-	12.0% (approx.)	1971	-
Sweden	0 – 2	29.0%	1967	45.0%	1971	+ 55%
Sweden	3 – 6	38.0%	1967	54.0%	1971	+ 42%
Switzerland	0 – 6	7.9%	1960	23.2%	1970	+ 201%
USA	0 – 5	20.2%	1960	31.4%	1971	+ 56%

Sources: Britain, Office of Population Censuses and Surveys (1973); 1961 and 71 Censuses;
Germany, Information supplied in correspondence from Statistisches Bundesamt;
Sweden, Swedish Joint Female Labour Council (1973);
United States, US Bureau of the Census (1972);
Austria, Netherlands and Switzerland, Census and other official statistical material forwarded in personal communications via embassies.

8: Employment rates of mothers with pre-school children in various local authority areas

Area	No. of employed married women with children under 5 per 1000 married women aged 15-44	Those employed over 30 hours a week per 1000 married women aged 15-44	Proportion of employed married women with children under 5, working over 30 hours a week
London			
Inner London Boroughs	99	42	42%
Brent, Ealing and Haringey	109	58	53%
Other Outer London Boroughs	70	23	33%
Six largest English County Boroughs (pre-1973)			
Birmingham	99	33	34%
Bristol	65	15	23%
Leeds	94	28	30%
Liverpool	87	23	27%
Manchester	107	38	36%
Sheffield	75	15	19%
Britain	80	23	29%

Sources: Unpublished data from 1971 Census (10% sample); 1971 Census Summary Tables (1% sample). The inclusion of married mothers only, and the calculation of employment rates using all married women aged 15-44, rather than just those with pre-school children, is due to the limitation of information available from the census.

Bibliography

Anderson, M. (1971) *Family Structure in Nineteenth-century Lancashire*, CUP, London

Beck, A. (1974) 'A Twenty-hour Week', *New Society*, 29, 493

Bereiter, C. (1972) 'An Academic Preschool for Disadvantaged Children: Conclusions from Evaluation Studies., in J.C. Stanley, (ed.) *Preschool Programs for the Disadvantaged*, Johns Hopkins University Press, Baltimore and London

Best, G. (1971) *Mid Victorian Britain 1851-75*, Weidenfeld & Nicolson, London

Blackstone, T. (1971) *A Fair Start: the Provision of Pre-School Education*, Allen Lane, London

Bloom, B. (1964) *Stability and Change in Human Characteristics*, Wiley, New York

Board of Education (1905) *Report of Children under five years of age in Public Elementary Schools by Women Inspectors*, Parliamentary Papers, 1905

— — (1908) *Report of a Consultative Committee on the School Attendance of Children below the Age of Five*, Parliamentary Papers, 1908, 82

Bowlby, J. (1951) *Maternal Care and Mental Health*, WHO, Geneva

Brablcová, V., Křivánek, F., and Matějček, J. (1974) *Czechoslovak Social Policy*, Orbis, Prague

Bronfenbrenner, U. (1974) *Report of Longitudinal Evaluations of Pre-school Programmes: Vol. 2, Is Early Intervention Effective?*, US Department of Health, Education and Welfare, Child Bureau

— — (1975) *The Challenge of Social Change to Public Policy and Developmental Research*, unpublished paper given at President's Symposium 'Child Development and Public Policy' at Annual Meeting of Society for Research in Child Development, 12 April 1975

Brown, G., Bhrolchain, M., and Harris, T., (1975) 'Social Class and Psychiatric Disturbance among Women in an Urban Population', *Sociology, 9*, 225-254

Burlingham, D., and Freud, A. (1944) *Infants without Families,* Allen & Unwin, London

Burnett, J. (1968) *Plenty and Want: A Social History of Diet in England from 1815 to the Present Day,* Penguin Books, London

Central Advisory Council for Education (England) (1967) *Children and their Primary Schools* (Plowden Report), HMSO, London

Central Statistical Office (1973) *Social Trends No. 4*, HMSO, London

— — (1974) *Social Trends No. 5*, HMSO, London

Chartered Institute of Public Finance and Accountancy (1974) *Local Health and Social Service Statistics 1972-73,* CIPFA and Society of County Treasurers, London

Chester, R. (1972) 'Current Incidence and Trends in Marital Breakdown', *Postgraduate Medical Journal, 48*, 529-541

Children's Community Centre (1974) *Our experiences of collective child care,* Children's Community Centre, 123 Dartmouth Park Hill, London N19

Clarke, A.M. and A.D.B. (eds) (1974) *Mental Deficiency, the changing outlook*, Methuen, London

Cole, G.D.H. and Postgate, R. (1948) *A History of the Common People*, Methuen, London

Comer, L. (1974) *Wedlocked Women*, Feminist Books, Leeds

Commission of the European Communities (1974) *The Employment of Women and the Problems it raises in the Member States of the European Community*, Office for Official Publications of the European Communities, Luxembourg

— — (1975) *Equality of Treatment between Men and Women Workers*, Brussels

Committee on the Care of Children (1946) *Report of the Committee* (Curtis Report), HMSO, London

Committee on Higher Education (1963) *Report of the Committee* (Robbins Report), HMSO, London

Committee on Local Authority and Allied Personal Social Services (1968) *Report of the Committee* (Seebohm Report), HMSO, London

Committee on One-Parent Families (1974) *Report of the Committee* (Finer Report), HMSO, London

Community Relations Commission (1974) *Educational Needs of Children from Minority Groups,* Community Relations Commission, London

Consultative Committee on Infant and Nursery Schools (1933) *Report of the Committee* (Hadow Report), HMSO, London

Curtis Report: see Committee on the Care of Children

Day, C. (1975) *Company Day Nurseries,* Institute of Personnel Management, London

Department of Education and Science (1972) *Education: A Framework for Expansion,* HMSO, London

— — (1974) *Educational Disadvantage and the Educational Needs of Immigrants:* Observations on the Report on Education of the Select Committee on Race Relations and Immigration, Cmnd 5720, HMSO, London

— — (1975a) *Statistics of Education 1973, Vol. I,* HMSO, London

— — (1975b) *Statistics of Education 1973, Vol. 5,* HMSO, London

— — (1975c) *Nursery Education* (DES Reports on Education No. 81), DES, London

Department of Health and Social Security (1971) *Two-Parent Families* (Statistical Report Series 14), HMSO, London

— — (1973) *Local Authority Social Services Statistics. Children's Day Care Facilities as at 31 March 1973,* DHSS, unpublished

— — (1974a) *The Family in Society: Preparation for Parenthood,* HMSO, London

— — (1974b) *The Family in Society: Dimensions of Parenthood,* HMSO, London

Engels, F. *(1968 edition) The Condition of the Working Class in England in 1844,* Allen & Unwin, London

Eversley, D. (1974) 'Population & Regional Planning', *New Society, 29,* 223-225

Expert Committee on Mental Health (1951) *Report on the Second Session,* Technical Report Series No. 31, WHO, Geneva.

Ferguson, S., and Fitzgerald, H. (1954) *Studies in the Social Services,* HMSO, London

Finer Report: See Committee on One-Parent Families

Fogarty, M., Rapoport, R. and R.N. (1971) *Sex, Career and Family,* Allen & Unwin, London

Foster, J. (1974) *Class Struggle and the Industrial Revolution,* Weidenfeld & Nicolson, London

Froebel, F. (1826) *The Education of Man,* (translated 1887, W.H. Hailmann), Appleton, New York

Gahagan, D.M. and G.A. (1970) *Talk Reform: explorations in language for infant school children,* Routledge & Kegan Paul, London

Gardner, D.E.M. (1948) *Testing Results in the Infant School,* Methuen, London

Gardner, D.E.M., and Cass, J. (1965) *The Role of the Teacher in the Infant and Nursery School,* Pergamon, London

Gavron, H. (1966) *The Captive Wife,* Routledge & Kegan Paul, London

Gathorne-Hardy, J. (1972) *The Rise and Fall of the British Nanny,* Hodder & Stoughton, London

Gilbert, B. (1966) *The Evolution of National Insurance in Great Britain,* Michael Joseph, London

Government Social Survey (1968) *A Survey of Women's Employment,* HMSO, London

Hadow Report: See Consultative Committee on Infant and Nursery Schools

Halsey, A.H. (ed.) (1972a) *Trends in British Society since 1900,* Macmillan, London

Halsey, A H. (1972b) *Educational Priority: EPA Problems and Policies,* Vol. I., HMSO, London

Heber, R., Garber H., Harrington, S., Hoffman, C., and Falender, C. (1972) *Rehabilitation of Families at Risk for Mental Retardation,* University of Wisconsin (duplicated report)

Heber, R. and Garber H. (1975) Progress Report II: 'An Experiment in The Prevention of Cultural-Familial Retardation' in *Proceedings of the Third Congress of the International Association for the Scientific Study of Mental Deficiency,* Polish Medical Publishers, Warsaw

Holt, J. (1975) *Escape from Childhood: the needs and rights of children,* Penguin Books, London

Hood, C., Oppé, T., Pless, I., and Apte, E. (1970) *Children of West Indian Immigrants*, Institute of Race Relations, London

Hunt, J. McV. (1961) *Intelligence and Experience*, Ronald Press, New York

Interdepartmental Committee on Physical Deterioration (1904) *Report on Physical Deterioration*, Parliamentary Papers 1904, *32*

Isaacs, S. (1930) *Intellectual Growth in Young Children*, Routledge, London

– – (1932) *The Nursery Years*, enlarged edition, Routledge, London

Klein, V. (1965) *Britain's Married Women Workers*, Routledge & Kegan Paul, London

Komorovsky, M. (1953) *Women in the Modern World*, Little Brown, Boston

Laslett, P. (1965) *The World we have Lost*, Methuen, London

Lomas, G. (1975) 'Race and Employment', *New Society*, *32* 413

McKeown, T. (1965) *Medicine in Modern Society*, Allen & Unwin, London

Miller, L.B., and Dyer, J.L. (1970) 'Experimental Variation of Head Start Curricula: A Comparison of Current Approaches', *Annual Progress Report, 1 June – 31 May 1970*, University of Louisville, Department of Psychology, Kentucky

Moss, P., Tizard, J., and Crook, J. (1973) 'Families and their Needs', *New Society*, *23*, 638-640.

Nandy, L, and D. (1975) 'Towards True Equality for Women', *New Society*, *31*, 246-249

Newson, J., and E. (1974) 'Cultural Aspects of Child-rearing in the English-speaking World', in *The Integration of a Child into a Social World*. (Richards, M., ed.), CUP, London

Nye, F., and Hoffman, L. (1963) *The Employed Mother in America*, Rand McNally, Chicago

Oakley, A. (1974a) *Housewife*, Allen Lane, London

– – (1974b) *Sociology of Housework*, Martin Robertson, London

Office of Population Censuses and Surveys (1973) *General Household Survey: General Introductory Report*, HMSO, London

240

— — (1975a) *Population Trends 1*, HMSO, London
— — (1975b) *Population Trends 2*, HMSO, London
Organisation for Economic Cooperation and Development (1972) *Working Documents. Programme Area I — Project I. Early Childhood Education.* OECD (unpublished)
— — (1973) 'Papers prepared for Meeting on Early Childhood Education, October 1973', OECD, Paris (unpublished)
— — (1974) 'Paper for a Working Party on the Role of Women in the Economy, OECD, Paris (unpublished)
Parry, M., and Archer, H. (1974) *Pre-School Education*, a Schools Council Research Study, Macmillan, London
Perkin, H. (1969) *The Origins of Modern English Society*, Routledge & Kegan Paul, London
Pinchbeck, I. and Hewitt, M. (1973) *Children in English Society, Vol. 2*, Routledge & Kegan Paul, London
Plowden Report: See Central Advisory Council for Education (England)
Pollak, M. (1972) *Today's Three Year Olds in London*, Heinemann, London
Richman, N. (1974) 'The Effects of Housing on Pre-School Children and their Mothers', *Developmental Medicine and Child Neurology, 16*, 53-58
Robbins Report: See Committee on Higher Education
Rosen, G. (1973) 'Disease, Debility & Death' in Dyos, H., and Wolfe, M. (eds) *The Victorian City, Vol. 2*, Routledge & Kegan Paul, London
Rosengren, B. (1973) *Pre-school in Sweden: Facts, Trends and Future*, Swedish Institute, Stockholm
Russell, B. (1934) *Freedom and Organisation 1814-1914*, Allen & Unwin, London
Rutter, M., Tizard, J., and Whitmore, K. (1970) (eds) *Education, Health and Behaviour*, Longmans, London
Rutter M. (1972) *Maternal Deprivation Reassessed*, Penguin Books, London
Rutter, M., Yule, W., Berger, M., Yule, B., and Bagley, C. (1974) 'Children of West Indian Immigrants — I. Rates of Behavioural Deviance and of Psychiatric Disorder', *Journal of Child Psychology and Psychiatry, 15*, 241-262
Rutter, M and Madge, N. (1976) *Cycles of Disadvantage* Heinemann, London

Seebohm Report: See Committee on Local Authority and Allied Personal Social Services

Spring-Rice, M. (1939) *Working-Class Wives,* Penguin Books, London

Stedman-Jones, G. (1971) *Outcast London,* OUP, London

Steiner, L. (1973) 'Why "Back to the Drawing Board" in Early Childhoood Education?', *Ideas, 26,* 2

Swedish Joint Female Labour Council (1973) *Women in Sweden in the Light of Statistics,* Arbetsmarknadens Kvinonand, Stockholm

Szabady, E. (1972) 'Impact of the New Child Care Allowances', *New Hungarian Quarterly, XIII, 48,* 99-110

Thompson, B. (1975) Adjustment to School, *Educational Research, 17,* 128-136

Thompson, E.J. (1974) *Recent Trends in Births and Deaths and National Projections,* GLC Research Memorandum 449, GLC, London

Thompson E.P. (1963) *The Makings of the English Working Class,* Victor Gollancz, London

Thompson, F. (1945) *Lark Rise to Candleford,* OUP, London

Titmuss, R. (1958) *Essays on the Welfare State,* Allen & Unwin, London

Tizard, B., Cooperman, O., Joseph, A., Tizard, J. (1972) 'Environmental Effects on Language Development: A Study of Young Children in Long-Stay Residential Nurseries', *Child Development, 43,* 337-358.

Tizard, B. (1975a) *Early Childhood Education: A Review and Discussion of Current Research in Britain,* NFER, Slough

— — (1975b) 'The Effect of Early Institutional Rearing on the Behaviour Problems and Affectional Relationships of Four-Year-Old Children', *Journal of Child Psychology and Psychiatry, 16,* 61-73

Tizard, B., Philps, J., Plewis, I. (1976) "Staff Behaviour in Pre-school Centres', *Journal of Child Psychology and Psychiatry,* in press

Tizard, J. (1974) 'Disadvantaged Children and Their Early Education', in Van Leer Foundation, *Curriculum in Early Childhood Education:* Report of a Seminar held from 15-25 November 1972 in Jerusalem, Bernard Van Leer Foundation, The Hague

Tizard, J. (1975) 'Issues in Early Childhood Education': Dorothy Gardner Lecture (given at the University of London Institute of Education, 3 May 1975), *Child Development Society Newsletter*. No. 24

Van der Eyken, W. (1974) *The pre-school years*, Penguin edition, London

Wedge, P and Prosser, H. (1973) *Born to Fail?*, Arrow Books in association with the National Children's Bureau, London

Whitbread, N. (1972) *The Evolution of the Nursery-Infant School*, Routledge & Kegan Paul, London

Willmott, P., and Young, M. (1957) *Family and Kinship in East London*, Routledge & Kegan Paul, London

Wilson, H., and Herbert, G.W. (1975) *Policy and Politics, 3*, No 2

Women's Cooperative Guild (1917) *Maternity*, Women's Cooperative Guild, London

Wynn, M. (1970) *Family Policy*, Michael Joseph, London

Yudkin, S. (1967) *0-5: A Report on the Care of Pre-School Children*, National Society of Children's Nurseries, London

Yudkin, S., and Holme, A. (1969) *Working Mothers and Their Children*, Sphere Books, London

Acknowledgements

We are grateful to the author, George Allen & Unwin Ltd, and Hafner Press for permission to use a diagram from *Medicine in Modern Society* by T. McKeown. We are also grateful to the following for permission to quote copyright material: to Methuen & Co. Ltd and the authors, G.D.H. Cole and R. Postgate for an extract from *The Common People, 1746-1946* (1948); to *The Times* for two articles; to Penguin Books Ltd for an extract from *Maternal Deprivation Re-assessed* by M. Rutter (1972); to A.D. Peters & Co. Ltd for an extract by Margaret Drabble in *Escape from Childhood: the Needs and Rights of Children* by J. Holt (1975) and to Penguin Books Ltd for a further extract from the same book; to George Allen & Unwin for an extract from *Freedom and Organisation* by B. Russell (1934); to George Routledge & Sons Ltd for an extract from *Intellectual Growth in Young Children* by Susan Isaacs (1930); to the International Association for the Scientific Study of Mental Deficiency for an extract from an article by R. Heber and H. Garber (1975); to *Ideas* and the author for an article by L. Steiner (1973); to Johns Hopkins University Press for an extract by C. Bereiter in *An Academic Preschool for Disadvantaged Children* (J.C. Stanley, ed., 1972); to Oxford University Press for an extract from *Lark Rise to Candleford* by F. Thompson (1945); to the Social Science Research Council for an extract from *Early Childhood Education: A Review and Discussion of Current Research in Britain* by Barbara Tizard; to Weidenfeld & Nicholson Ltd for an extract from *Class Struggle & the Industrial Revolution* by J. Foster (1974); to Methuen & Co. Ltd and the author for an extract from *The World We Have Lost* by P. Laslett (1965); to George Allen & Unwin Ltd for an extract from *Sex, Career & Family* by Fogarty, Rapoport and Rapoport (1971).

Index

services 35-6; nutrition 35; poverty 31-5, 48; school meals 47;
urbanisation 30
Norway, pre-school provision 118
Nursery Centres Scheme 71
nursery classes: ages of children 98-100, 108; description 94; numbers
(1973) 92
nursery education (see also nursery schools, nursery classes, pre-school
provision): attitude of authorities and government 65-6, 76;
attitude of parents 62-3; coordination with day care in second
world war 72; cost and staffing 108-9; effect of current economic
situation 89-90; effects of nursery education 171-2, 181-3, 185,
191-3; enjoyment of children 27; exclusion of two year olds 85;
expansion outlined in White Paper 84; objections 162; part time
policy 102-3; purpose and content 25-6, 174-81, 183, 206;
regional variations 107-8; views of Hadow Committee 70; views of
Plowden Committee 82-4, 160-3
nursery—infant schooling: attitude of Board of Education 62-6; effects
of Revised Code (1862) 56; history and development (to 1914)
52-7; payment by results 56-7; post-war plans 75; right of
admission for under fives 62; rise and fall in numbers (to 1930)
61- 2, 69; under fives at school in nineteenth century 57-8
nursery schools (see also nursery education, nursery classes): ages of
children attending 98-100, 108; description of services 94; direct
grant and independent 97; exceptions 81; expansion (in 1930s) 70;
foundation of 43, 52; full time provision 102; growth in private
sector 78; Hadow Committee views 70; justification 161; numbers
during second world war 72, 74; numbers (in 1966) 81; (in 1973)
88; official recommendation of separate system 64; places created
under Urban Aid Programme 84; post-war plans 75

one-parent families: children of, in day nurseries 104; children under
five 15, 102; percentage in labour force 130,144; rise in numbers 15
Owen, Robert 52-4; curriculum for schools 52-3; ideas about nursery
schooling 52; opposition towards 53

parents (see also roles, family): attitudes to nursery schooling, early
twentieth century 62-3; contribution to cost of day nurseries 109;
involvement in child upbringing 28; involvement in intervention
programmes 202-4; involvement in organised care 217, 223-5;
relationship with professional workers 24-5; rights in nineteenth
century 47
part-time nursery groups: run by local authority 93
part-time provision: amount and description 101-4; introduction of
part-time nursery schooling 76, 102; Plowden's endorsement 82,
143; policy in nursery education 102, 143-5

Pestalozzi 53

play: its importance in Froebel's system 60-1; psycho-analytical justification 179-81; role in nursery education 174-8

playgroups: as middle-class institution 79; description 95-6; history and growth 76-9; numbers (in 1972) 78; regional variation 106-7

Plowden Report 175-86; attitudes to working mothers 142-4; conclusions on nursery education 82-4; demand for pre-school provision 83, 160-3

population: growth in nineteenth century 31; movement 106

poverty: among families with young children 146-7; attempts to combat 35; in nineteenth century 31-6

Pre-school Playgroups Association 78

pre-school provision: ages of children 97-100; arguments against 27; as part of a family policy 213; availability 137, 215-16; benefits 27; best care for under threes 82-3, 219; case for expansion 26-8; coordination of services 121, 214; contribution of child-minders 221-3; costs and staffing 108-11; demand 57-8, 62-3, 83, 102, 137-9, 160-5; different services 93-7; effects of providing 138-9; exceptions (in 1960s) 81; full or part-time 101-4; guide lines for development 213-17; importance of choice 26-7, 215-16, 219; in Europe 112-21; need for private provision 75; numbers (in 1973) 88, 92; parental involvement 59, 217, 223-5; post-Seebohm expansion 87-8; provision of medical service 216-17; social class of children 104; unresolved issues 219-26; world-wide expansion 12-13

primary schools: ages of under fives 98; classes for under fives 94; expansion of nursery classes 84; under fives (in 1947) 74; (in 1973) 92

private nurseries: description 95-6; regional pattern 106

private pre-school provision: description and regulations 95-7; growth of 'nursery schools' 78; need 75; numbers (in 1966) 81; (in 1973) 88, 92; role in European countries 112-13, 121

professional workers: influence on child upbringing 24-6; relationship with parents 24

regional variations: married womens' employment 39-40; mothers' employment 127-9, 134-5; part-time nursery groups 93; spending on day nurseries 88-9; types of pre-school provision 104-8

relatives: to look after children 136-7

Revised Code, 1862: effects on infant schooling 56-7; payments system 56-7

rising fives: definition 94; numbers in school 98-100

Robbins Report 182

roles, of parents: changing views 22-4; effect of mothers' employment 155; importance of choice 26-7; segregation 67, 207; sharing and equality with family 26-7, 152, 210-13

rural areas: level of day nursery provision 105; working mothers 39, 129

Other books in the series

towards a NEW SOCIETY

RACE, INTELLIGENCE AND EDUCATION
H.J. Eysenck
SEX, GENDER AND SOCIETY
Ann Oakley
STORIES FROM THE DOLE QUEUE
Tony Gould & Joe Kenyon (out of print)
THE VILLAGE IN THE CITY
Nicholas Taylor
LONELINESS
Jeremy Seabrook (out of print)
IN PLACE OF PRISON
Dennie Briggs

New Society comes out weekly, containing articles by experts on sociology, anthropology, psychology, the social services, government, planning, education, and other matters of social concern.

It always contains: social policy notes; current research results; reviews of books; and reviews of the arts. The articles are written with intelligence, concern and clarity about subjects that can often be fogged by jargon.

New Society is available from newsagents on Thursdays, or by direct subscription from 128 Long Acre, London WC2.